Christmas
IN THE
TRENCHES

Christmas
IN THE
TRENCHES

ALAN WAKEFIELD

The History Press

Front cover: Officers of the Royal Field Artillery with their Christmas mail bag, December 1917 (*Q 8346, Imperial War Museum*).
Back cover: Top to bottom, Christmas card produced by the 53rd Battalion, Australian Imperial Force, 1918. *(Private Collection).* Christmas card produced for the 56th (London) Division, 1917. *(Private Collection).*

First published in 2006
This edition published in 2010

The History Press
The Mill, Brimscombe Port
Stroud, Gloucestershire, GL5 2QG
www.thehistorypress.co.uk

British Library Cataloguing in Publication Data.
A catalogue record for this book is available from the British Library.

ISBN 978 0 7524 5807 6

Typesetting and origination by The History Press
Printed in Great Britain

Contents

Acknowledgements

I would like to take the opportunity to thank a number of people whose assistance made the research for and writing of this book a relatively straightforward task. Firstly, Anthony Richards of the Imperial War Museum's Department of Documents, who not only kept up with my call for collections of letters and diaries, but also took on the task of proof-reading the first draft of my manuscript. I would also like to thank Gavin Birch who, working with acquisitions in the Imperial War Museum's Photograph Archive, kept me informed of the arrival of new illustrative material. From other national museums I have to acknowledge the assistance of Simon Moody from the National Army Museum's Department of Archives, Photographs, Film and Sound, who led me to a number of interesting collections, which complemented those from the IWM, and Nina Burls from the RAF Museum's Department of Research and Information Services for helping me access the Roscoe collection. Staff of the National Archives must also be thanked for facilitating access to the battalion, brigade and divisional war diaries in their charge.

Access to the written and illustrative material is only half the story and I acknowledge the permission given by copyright holders to reproduce material in this book, without which the project could not have been completed. Alongside the numerous individual copyright holders are the Trustees of the Imperial War Museum and the Director and Council of the National Army Museum, who hold copyright over a number of the accounts used in the book and, in the case of the former, almost all of the illustrations. Similar thanks must go to Harrods Ltd for granting permission to reproduce advertisements from catalogues dating from the First World War. I was kindly assisted in accessing material held by Harrods by company archivist Sebastian Wormell.

The following individuals also deserve a mention either for loaning me original material or for their kind offers of support and encouragement; John and Tony Begg, Malcolm Brown, Anna De, Bruce Dennis, Francis Mackay and Peter Saunders. Finally, I would like to thank my wife Julie for assisting with the selection of photographs for the book and for putting up with losing me to the computer on numerous evenings and weekends.

Willow Trench in the Rue de Bois sector, December 1914. The flooding of this trench played a part in the informal truce on this part of the front line at Christmas 1914. *'There was a frost yesterday but it is thawing now and the water is rising in the trench, though the boards along the bottom enable you to walk along dry shod – comparatively; you get a bootful occasionally.' (Rfm J. Selby Grigg, 1/5th Londons) (Q 56198)*

Introduction

The outbreak of war in August 1914 was generally greeted by the peoples of the European great powers with enthusiasm and euphoria. Patriotism surged through the nations of Europe and a sense of national unity manifested itself even in countries such as Austria-Hungary and Russia, where deep-seated political and social divisions existed that had not long before looked likely to split these nations apart or lead to civil war and revolution. Instead, political ceasefires were called as everyone lined up behind the governments and ruling elites of the day. Both war planners, political leaders and the populace at large believed the war would be short and victorious for their side. In any case, many believed that it would be impossible for modern industrial nations to fight a long war because of the disruption this would bring to their economies, which were linked in a highly interdependent system of international trade. Few had the foresight to see that once the resources of modern industrial states were fully harnessed for war a very different outcome could follow.

In Britain the phrase 'all over by Christmas' was much uttered, and similar stock phrases could no doubt be found for the other warring nations. However, there would be almost another four wartime Christmases to follow that first one before the conflict was resolved. The war grew to encompass the Mediterranean, Middle East and Africa and became a more industrialised and intensive conflict through the ever growing use of artillery and the introduction of such weapons as gas, tanks and purpose-built bombing aircraft. Through all this the citizen soldier, who made up the bulk of most of the armies, whether he be a volunteer, conscript or reservist recalled to the colours, found solace in many of the simple things in life that could, even for a short time, take his mind off the situation in which he found himself and brought forward thoughts of home, family and life before the war. Christmas, an important annual celebration and holiday in many of the combatant nations, provided an obvious opportunity for troops to focus on something other than the war. Although birthdays and other personal celebrations provided important links with home and a chance for soldiers to celebrate, the 'national' and 'international' status of Christmas allowed for large-scale festivities involving whole battalions or regiments. Such activities, generally taking place behind the lines when units were on rest, were encouraged by the High Command as morale-boosting exercises; the troops were given time off, plentiful food and drink and organised activities such as sport and concerts.

If sharing Christmas cheer with your comrades and allies was actively supported by the military authorities, then attempts to share the compliments of the season with the enemy was viewed with great alarm by senior officers and war leaders as they feared their troops' fighting spirit would be undermined by fraternising and temporary truces with the enemy. Following the events of the now famous Christmas Truce of 1914, extensively covered in the excellent book by Malcolm Brown and Shirley Seaton,[1] much effort was expended to prevent such contacts being established again. Although these worked to a large extent, limited open contacts with the enemy and a whole system of more covert trucing, which became known as the 'live and let live' system, developed between soldiers sharing the same conditions and hardships in the front line.[2]

Through the use of photographs, illustrations and the words of soldiers themselves this book will attempt to give a flavour of how Christmas was celebrated by British forces during the First World War. The objective is to look beyond the 1914 Christmas Truce, by covering the following four years and the experiences of those serving in theatres of war beyond France and Flanders, such as Gallipoli, Italy, Mesopotamia, Palestine and Salonika. In this way the book provides a glimpse of the different Christmas experiences a soldier could have during the four years of war. There are accounts by those serving behind the lines, the wounded in hospital, prisoners of war, men training in Great Britain and those on garrison duty in that jewel in the crown of the British Empire, India.

Nursing staff and patients in 'The Hut' ward at the Radcliffe Infirmary, Oxford (3rd General Southern Hospital), Christmas 1915. *(7702-15)*

Christmas 1918 is also included as many troops were still overseas awaiting demobilisation, on duty with forces of occupation in Germany, Turkey, Bulgaria and parts of the former Austro-Hungarian Empire or fighting against the Bolsheviks in various parts of Russia. This qualifies it very much as a 'wartime' Christmas and thus worthy of inclusion here. Each year of the war is given a chapter in which an overview of the progress of the conflict provides the background against which the words of the soldiers and illustrative material tell the story of Christmas in the trenches from 1914 to 1918.

Each first-hand account used in this book is referenced by the individual's name and unit and the repository in which the material is held. Footnotes cover only published works or where a specific letter or other document from a larger collection has been cited. In the text, each account is accompanied by the name of the individual or unit to which it relates. All ranks and unit designations used relate to the time of the events described. Unless stated otherwise, illustrative material comes from the Photographs Archive and Department of Documents at the Imperial War Museum.

The First Christmas: 1914

In offering to the Army in France my earnest and most heartfelt good wishes for Xmas and the New Year, I am anxious once more to express the admiration I feel for the valour and endurance they have displayed throughout the campaign and to assure them that to have commanded such magnificent troops in the field will be the proudest remembrance of my life.

Sir John French's Special Order of the Day, issued to the BEF,

25 December 1914

In December 1914, the British Expeditionary Force (BEF) was holding a line some 30 miles in length from St Eloi, just south of Ypres, down to Givenchy on the La Bassée Canal. Crossing much of the area was a system of drainage ditches and watercourses that prevented this low-lying land from flooding. Unfortunately, artillery fire and the construction of trenches had damaged much of this network with the result that, once the winter weather arrived, the area began to be transformed into a morass. The hastily dug trenches offered little in the way of comfort:

I have just come out of 2 days and 2 nights in the trenches. I wonder how many people realize what the trenches are like. In some newspapers one sees accounts of hot soup and wonderful fires etc. In some places the mud came over my knees. This is not exaggerated. In most places over ones ankles. The first night it was horrid, raining all night. No room to move. It is really wonderful what the Tommy stands . . . You should have seen us coming out – all mud from head to foot, sore feet and heavy equipment. But are we downhearted? Not one![1] (*2/Lt Wilbert Spencer, 2nd Wiltshires*)

As both sides struggled to keep their trenches dry the intensity of trench fighting died down and small-scale ad hoc truces began to occur in some sectors of the line with both sides refraining from firing during mealtimes and at ration-carrying parties. Following spells of the worst weather, small working parties on each side could be observed working in the open repairing trenches and breastworks with little interference from those on the 'other side of the wire'. The closeness and constant presence of the enemy in trench warfare bred a curiousness and realisation that the enemy was suffering exactly the same conditions. Through this the 'live and let live system' started to develop, whereby many opposing units made daily life more bearable by reducing the general level of violence:

> Things up here are very quiet – in my part of the line the trenches are only 50 or 60 yards apart in places, and we can hear the Germans talking. They often shout to us in English and we respond with cries of 'waiter'. There was one fellow who had a fire with a tin chimney sticking up over the parapet and our men were having shots at it with their rifles. After each shot the German waved a stick or rang a bell according to whether we hit the chimney or not! There are lots of amusing incidents up there and altogether we have quite a cheery time our worst trouble is the wet and mud which is knee-deep in some places.[2] (*2/Lt Dougan Chater, 2nd Gordon Highlanders*)

This is not to say that troops were guaranteed a quiet time in the line. Artillery bombardments still fell on occasion, although a shell shortage generally confined heavy gunfire to offensive operations and trench raids. Of greater concern were snipers who, during this relatively quiet period, were usually waiting to account for the unwary and the careless. At Fleurbaix for example:

> These snipers seldom missed. Their guns were fixed during the day to aim at a certain spot, and then during the hours of darkness they would fire at short irregular intervals, hoping to catch some of us who were moving about. Shallow parts of the trench and the holes in the convent wall immediately behind us were their favourite targets.

Lt G.J. Grant (foreground) and men of the 2nd Argyll & Sutherland Highlanders are constructing breastworks in No Man's Land during the informal Christmas Truce with German troops in the Rue de Bois sector of the line. The German front line ran in front of the trees on the left of the photograph. *'Looking down towards the trenches it was just like Earls Court Exhibition. There were the two sets of front trenches only a few yards apart, and yet there were soldiers, both British and German, standing on the top of them, digging or repairing the trench in some way, without even shooting at each other.'* (*2/Lt Cyril Drummond, RFA*) (Q 56199)

Working and ration parties used to congregate behind the wall, owing to the communication trenches being full of water, and woe betide anyone who forgot for a moment and in the darkness stood in a gap in the wall instead of actually behind it . . . (*Pte W.A. Quinton, 2nd Bedfords*)

With the realisation that they would still be on active service over Christmas, the soldiers' thoughts naturally turned to home and to how they could best celebrate the festive season under such trying circumstances:

I should like the pudding sent off soon or else it may not reach me in time for Christmas. I don't know whether I shall be able to eat it on

Christmas Day or not, it all depends on whether we happen to be in the trenches or not on that day. If we are not we will have pheasant and the puddings which will be very near the ordinary Christmas fare except for the company and the decorations but still we shall have to institute another Christmas when we come back and have all the festivities over again.[3] (*Rfm Richard Lintott, 1/5th Londons*)

Parcels and Christmas gifts would not only come from families and friends; regimental associations, counties, towns and cities also supplied their fighting men with useful articles. Rfm Lintott, for example, received three khaki handkerchiefs, a tin of Abdullah cigarettes, a cigarette lighter and writing paper from the people of Horsham and a ½ lb tin of butter, a tin of milk, a tin of cocoa, a handkerchief and a case of writing material from his regiment. Among the gifts came one of the most enduring mementos of the First World War, the Princess Mary Gift Box. This was to be given to all those wearing the King's uniform on Christmas Day 1914: some 2,620,019 men in total. With such a huge number of gift boxes and their contents to be manufactured, distribution priority was given to members of the BEF in France and the Royal Navy. In total some 426,724 boxes were received on Christmas Day, the remainder being issued subsequently.[4] That this gift, along with a Christmas card from the King and Queen, was appreciated by the troops is shown by the mentions it receives in letters, diaries and memoirs as well as the fact that many men repacked the tins and sent them home to their families for safe keeping.

The arrival of Princess Mary's gift coincided with one of the most widely known events of the war, the Christmas Truce. Until the evening of 24 December the weather had been generally very wet. However Christmas Eve brought a sharp frost, causing the ground to harden and thus easing mobility, a factor that would prove important the following day. As Christmas drew near even headquarters slackened their workloads; for example, at 4th Division HQ a communication was sent out to all units stating that owing to Christmas the divisional signals service would only deal with priority messages during the night of 25–26 December.[5] For British troops in many parts of the line, strange activity on the part of the Germans soon became apparent:

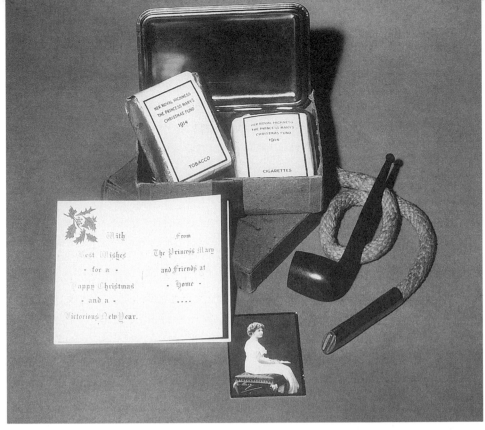

The Princess Mary's Gift tin for smokers was distributed to soldiers and sailors over Christmas 1914. The contents were one ounce of pipe tobacco, a packet of 20 cigarettes, a pipe, a tinder lighter, Christmas card and photograph of the Princess. *(MH 30527)*

The Princess Mary's Gift tin for non-smokers was distributed to soldiers and sailors over Christmas 1914 and contained a packet of acid drops, a khaki writing case with pencil, paper and envelopes as well as a Christmas card and photograph of the Princess. *(MH 30528)*

The brass tin in which soldiers and sailors received their gift from Princess Mary's Christmas Fund in 1914. Apart from the smokers' and non-smokers' gifts, it was also decided to produce special gift sets for Indian troops. Gurkhas received the same boxes as their British counterparts, Sikhs were given a box of sweets, a tin box of spices and a Christmas card, while all other Indian troops received the tin with a packet of 20 cigarettes, some sugar candy, a tin box of spices and the Christmas card. *(MH 30529)*

As darkness came on lights were seen in the German lines in the Rue du Bois, at first our fellows fired at them and the Germans put them out – gradually the firing died down, and all the enemy sniping ceased. The silence was almost uncanny and we were all very suspicious and extra vigilant, expecting some trick. Later on lights began to appear in the German trenches and their whole line was illuminated. I think they had hoisted lanterns on tall poles on their parapet and in their trenches. After that they began to sing . . . finishing up with the Wacht am Rhein, the German and Austrian national anthems. They sang beautifully the whole effect was weird in the extreme. They then started shouting remarks across to us which we replied, but I could not hear what was said. I think everyone felt very homesick on Xmas Eve. Thoughts of our families at home were uppermost in our minds.

The night passed without a shot being fired on either side. Our sentries were however extra vigilant and I felt quite uneasy at the strange silence. (*Maj Q. Henriques, 1/16th Londons*)

The activity opposite the 1/16th Londons stopped some men from the battalion giving the Germans a special seasonal gift:

We had decided to give the Germans a Christmas present of 3 carols and 5 rounds rapid. Accordingly as soon as night fell we started and the strains of 'While Shepherds' (beautifully rendered by the choir) arose upon the air. We finished that and paused preparatory to giving the 2nd item on the programme, but lo! We heard answering strains arising from *their* lines. Also they started shouting across to us. Therefore we stopped any hostile operations and commenced to shout back. One of them shouted 'A Merry Christmas English, we're not shooting tonight'. We yelled back a similar message and from that time on until we were relieved on Boxing morning at 4am not a shot was fired. After this shouting had gone on for some time they stuck up a light. Not to be out done so did we. Then up went another, so we shoved up another. Soon the two lines looked like an illuminated fete. Opposite me they had one lamp and 9 candles in a row. And we had all the candles and lights we could muster stuck on our bayonets above the parapet. At 12.00 we sang 'God save the King' and with the exception of the sentries turned in.[6] (*Rfm Ernest Morley, 1/16th Londons*)

With generally friendly relations established through the previous evening's verbal advances the scene was set for the more adventurous souls on each side to move the truce to another level:

On Christmas Day the Germans stuck up a white light and shouted that if we refrained from firing they would do the same. We did so and people started showing themselves over the trenches and waving to each other. Shortly 2 Germans advanced unarmed towards our trenches and our men did the same. They met ½ way and shook hands, exchanged cigarettes and cigars and souvenirs and soon there was quite a big crowd

Riflemen Andrew and Grigg (1/5th Londons) with Saxons of the 104th and 106th Regiments at Ploegsteert on Christmas Day 1914. '*We found our enemies to be Saxons. . . . I raked up some of my rusty German and chatted with some of them. None of them seemed to have any personal animosity against England and all said they would be fully glad when the war was over. Turner took some snaps with his pocket camera, copies of which I hope you will eventually see.*' (*Rfm J. Selby Grigg, 1/5th Londons*) (*Q 70075*)

between the trenches, we 3 included. Russell was introduced to a barber in the Strand named Liddle (spelling phonetic). Another German asked Russell in good English if he would like to go home. Russell asked him where he lived and the chap said London and hoped he would soon be able to return there. Both sides then buried the dead whom they had been unable to get at before, after which the Germans were ordered back to their trenches. Both sides continued to expose themselves, however, and to hold amiable conversations, and when we were relieved this morning not a shot had been fired on either side in our trenches though we could hear firing on both flanks and the artillery were bombarding each other over our heads.[7] (*Rfm Jack Chappell, 1/5th Londons*)

In some sectors the need to bury the dead was a central factor in the truce taking place. Near Frelinghien, the 2nd Monmouthshire Regiment were holding the line:

British and German officers and men fraternising on Christmas Day in No Man's Land at Rue Pétillon, scene of the costly attack by the 20th Brigade on 18–19 December. On this sector of the line it was the need to bury the dead that initiated the trucing. *'All Christmas Day we were walking about outside in front of our trenches. The Germans came out of theirs and we met half way and talked and exchanged souvenirs, our bullets for theirs. They also gave some of our fellows cigars of which they said they had plenty and we gave them tins of bully beef as they said they had very little food.' (Pte Warwick Squire, 1/13th Londons) (Q 50719)*

Just imagine our feelings when we thought of home and looked out at our bleak surroundings. A yard or so from where I was standing a German soldier had been buried, and his foot had actually been sticking out in our trench until we had covered it up with earth. The stench at times was almost unbearable. (*Sgt Francis Brown*)

In some places the opposing troops joined together in paying their respects to the dead:

Near where we were standing a dead German who had been brought in by some of the English was being buried and a German officer after reading a short service in German, during which both English and Germans uncovered [their heads, he said], 'We thank our English

British and German troops in No Man's Land burying the dead from the attack put in by the 20th Brigade on 18–19 December. British units involved in the truce on this sector (Sailly–Fromelles Road) included the Northumberland Hussars and 55th Field Company, R.E. Matters were very similar on the adjacent La Boutillerie sector: '*I went out and found that they were willing to have an armistice for 4 hours, and to carry our dead men back halfway for us to bury. A few days previous we had had an attack with many losses. This I arranged, and then – can you imagine it – both sides came out, met in the middle, shook hands, wished each other the compliments of the season and had a chat. A strange sight between two hostile lines. They then carried over the dead. I won't describe the sights I saw and which I shall never forget. We buried the dead as they were.*' (*2/Lt Wilbert Spencer, 2nd Wiltshires*) (*Q 50720*)

friends for bringing in our dead' and then said something in broken English about a Merry Xmas and Happy New Year. They stuck a bit of wood over the grave – no name on it only 'Vor Vaterland und Freheit' (for Fatherland and Freedom). After a little while the German officers called their men in and we went back to our breastworks, calling in at a shelled out estaminet on the way to loot a chair and one or two other articles.[8] (*Rfm Selby Grigg, 1/5th Londons*)

Although cordial relations were established across No Man's Land in many places, the truce was not universal and casualties were therefore inevitable. One of these unfortunate men was Sgt Frank Collins of the 2nd Monmouthshires:

About 8am voices could be heard shouting on our right front, where the trenches came together to about 35 yards apart, German heads appeared, and soon our fellows showed themselves and seasonal greetings were bawled back and forth, evidently Xmas feeling asserting itself on both sides. Presently a Sergt. Collins of my Regiment stood waist high above the trench waving a box of Woodbines above his head. German soldiers beckoned him over, and Collins got out and walked half way towards them, in turn beckoning for someone to come and take the gift. However, they called out 'prisoner' and immediately Collins edged back the way he had come. Suddenly a shot rang out, and the poor Sergt. staggered back into the trench, shot through the chest. I can still hear his cries 'Oh my God, they have shot me', and he died immediately. (*Sgt Francis Brown*)

Despite the bitterness caused by the shooting, the truce held on the Monmouthshires' sector of the line and at 9 a.m. Welshmen and Bavarians exchanged gifts and season's greetings, with many of the Germans apologising for the shooting. Sgt Collins now lies in Calvaire (Essex) Military Cemetery, Comines-Warneton, 16km from Ypres on the road to Wijtschate and Ploegsteert.

After Boxing Day, although meetings in No Man's Land became rarer, opposing troops who had fraternised maintained the 'live and let live' attitude, with little in the way of hostilities. In places it was even arranged to have another truce on New Year's Day, 2/Lt Chater remarking in a letter to his mother that the Germans requested this in order to see how photographs taken on Christmas Day had turned out.[9] For Germans, New Year brought the feast day of St Sylvester, a traditional family holiday. However, one German practice of welcoming in the New Year did lead to some misunderstanding:

. . . things went smoothly till the night of the 31st. New Year's Eve. On this night we decided to remove our M.G. to a new position some couple of hundred yards or so along the trench, as we had a notion that the Germans knew of its present position, and would not hesitate to shell us out as soon as hostilities recommenced. Having prepared the

Photograph taken by 2/Lt Cyril Drummond (135th Battery, RFA) on Boxing Day near St Yvon north of Ploegsteert Wood, where men of the 2nd Royal Dublin Fusiliers truced with the Germans over Christmas 1914. *'We talked, mainly in French, because my German was not very good, and none of the Germans could speak English well. But we managed to get together alright. They were very nice fellows to look at, they looked more like university students than soldiers, and one of them said "We don't want to kill you, and you don't want to kill us. So why shoot?" . . . We talked about various subjects connected with the war and one of the Germans said something about dum dum bullets . . . We didn't pursue that subject. I lined them all up and took a photograph.' (2/Lt Cyril Drummond)* (HU 35801)

new gun-pit the previous night, we now made ready for the moving, and still being on friendly terms with the enemy, and our trenches being knee-deep in mud and water, we took the easiest course and travelled along the top behind our own trench. We started off, well loaded with all our kit, the gun, tripod, and boxes of belt ammunition, and our rifles slung across our backs by the slings. We made very slow progress as the ground was very heavy with mud (the snow having thawed) and in addition to this we had to negotiate the communication trenches that ran at right-angles to the firing-line. These were about 4ft wide and we crossed by taking a sort of staggering leap, and throwing the heavy stuff across to the outstretched arms of those already over.

An hour had passed and we had covered about three-parts of the total distance, when without a word of warning something happened that caused us to fall as one man, flat on our stomachs in the mud. The Germans had opened fire! Rifles and machine guns cracked. They had done the dirty on us! We crouched there in the mud, and the names we called those Germans must have turned the air blue. Yet, strange, we could not feel the 'pinging' of any bullets around us? The explanation came in the next few moments, when a voice from our front-line yelled 'Hi you fellows, what's up? They ain't firing across 'ere. They warned us what they were going to do. They're firing in the air to celebrate the coming-in of the New Year.' . . . Having made sure that the voice from the trench had spoken the truth, we staggered to our feet and continued our journey. How easily mistakes can be made! Being out of the trench we did not know of this midnight arrangement, and it was

Men of the 1/5th Londons just after their Christmas dinner in Ploegsteert Wood, 1914. *'We spent Christmas Eve and Christmas Day in some breastworks in the woods in support. My Christmas dinner consisted of stewed rabbit, rashers and Christmas pudding which was not so bad under the circumstances.' (Rfm Richard Lintott, 1/5th Londons) (Q 11729)*

lucky for the Germans that we had not misunderstood their intentions, and opened fire on them with our machine gun. This certainly would have broken up the temporary armistice.

And so this unofficial armistice with the enemy still held good. (*Pte W.A. Quinton*)

When news of the truce reached senior officers there was something of a mixed reaction. A report of IV Corps operations between 22 and 31 December 1914 records that German overtures for a temporary halt to hostilities were not entertained by the 8th Division, whereas the Gen Officer Commanding (GOC) 7th Division, Maj Gen Sir Thompson Capper, sanctioned the continuation of the truce on 26 and 27 December to allow adequate time for burial of the dead and drainage of watercourses and trenches, so as to improve the condition of the front line, the proviso being that no unit was to arrange any further formal or informal truce without reference to Corps HQ.[10] Once such work was completed, commanders on both sides realised they had to get the war started again before the fighting spirit of their men was permanently affected. On the German side an army order of 29 December declared that any act of fraternisation with the enemy would be treated as high treason. Similar, though less dramatic, was Gen Sir Horace Smith-Dorrien's 2nd Army instruction stating that any officer or NCO allowing informal understandings with the enemy would be tried by court martial. With orders arriving to begin vigorous artillery bombardment, sniping and machine gunning of the enemy, soldiers realised this brief interlude in the war was almost over. Some, however, were determined to ease their way back into the war, causing as little harm as possible to their new 'friends' on the other side of the wire:

The war was becoming a farce and the high-ups decided that this truce must stop. Orders came through to our Brigade, and so to my battery, that fire was to be opened the following morning on a certain farm which stood behind the German support line. Our battery was to put twelve rounds of high explosive shell into it at eleven o'clock. As luck would happen, I was the officer who would have to do this. So I said

Men of the 2nd Scots Guards digging out a trench near the Rue Pétillon, 19 November 1914. *'The mud is awful. Everything is mud and we are just lumps of mud. In parts of our trenches the mud comes up to one's thighs, soft slushy mud and in others sticky clingy mud over one's knees. I've had quite enough of mud. With mud, love and best wishes for the New Year to you all.' (Pte Warwick Squire, 1/13th Londons) (Q 57380)*

to Johnny Hawkesley, 'What are we going to do? They'll all be there having coffee at eleven o'clock! I see them every morning from my O.P. through my telescope.' So he said 'Well, we've got to do it, so you'd better go up and talk to the Dubs about it.'

I went up and saw Colonel Loveband, who commanded the Dublin Fusiliers, and he sent someone over to tell the Boches, and the next morning at eleven o'clock I put twelve 18s into the farmhouse, and of course there wasn't anybody there. But that broke the truce – on our front at least. (*2/Lt Cyril Drummond, 32nd Brigade, RFA*)

From evidence in brigade, divisional and corps war diaries of the BEF for December 1914 it is obvious that a number of officers feared censure over the truce. Indeed, Smith-Dorrien had threatened action over reports of trucing that he learnt of on Boxing Day. Therefore reports sent up to senior commanders for the Christmas period stressed the usefulness of the truce as an intelligence-gathering exercise:

Germans making a great deal of noise last night singing and shouting. Some came towards our line and called for our men to go over to them. Two or three men went over and spoke to them and got quite close to their trenches. They reported farm S of LA of LA DOUVE occupied with considerable number of Germans round it and a number more singing east of avenue. Some of them are reported to have been wearing picklehaubes mostly caps or woollen helmets and some khaki covered shakos. Regtl number on shoulder thought to be 10 and 25.

Men of the 2nd Royal Scots Fusiliers in the line at La Boutillerie, winter 1914–15. This battalion relieved the 2nd Wiltshires on 27 December, so missing out on active participation in the Christmas Truce. *'Think of your old pal sleeping on a waterproof sheet laid on the wet clay, with all his clothes and overcoat on – both of which are sodden with clay – and covered with a soaking wet blanket. Its an absolute fact that when we came out of the trenches I, with the help of another, rang the water out of my blanket and my overcoat, when dry, stood up by itself! Still, while I envy you I do not grudge you your comfort. Be as comfortable as you can while you can.' (Rfm Ernest Morley, 1/16th Londons) (Q 49104)*

This morning several came up towards our trenches in the mist but were ordered back and warned that they would be fired at. Their Regtl numbers were 7 with green facings and shako, 134 with red facings and 10 with red facing, both the latter with caps. No helmets were seen. Reported that no wire between us and them that we cannot see. No firing at all today. R E wired right across left section last night. We have been wiring and cleaning up in the mist. (*Report from 2nd Seaforth Highlanders, 10th Infantry Brigade to HQ 4th Division*)[11]

Along with regimental identifications came information on the age and apparent fitness of enemy troops, the strength in which they were holding the front line, the state of the enemy's trenches, locations of machine guns and sniping positions. It was even recorded that a Lt Belcher of the 1st East Lancashires talked with a sniper, asking him where he generally fired from so that he could have a pot at him, but the man was not fool enough to give the show away.[12] General information gleaned from German newspapers, exchanged during the truce, was also sent up the chain of command as evidence of German morale at home and attitudes towards the British.

The High Command need not have worried about the truce developing into a general 'soldiers' peace' as the overwhelming majority of those taking part regarded it simply as a festive interlude in a war that needed to be won. Lt Col Rupert Shoolbred (1/16th Londons), writing to his brother Walter in a German prisoner-of-war camp, stated:

Some people have different opinions as to the rightness or wrongness of this informal Xmas truce – personally I do not see that it can do anything but good, and that the more widely it is known the better it will be. It enabled our people and those opposite them likewise to discover that they are both human beings, and though now again we are each doing all we can against each other, I hope many will do it without the same feeling of personal enmity that probably was in many cases present before. I do not think a man need fight any worse for recognizing that his enemy is a man like himself and of the same home love and all the thousand other kindred feelings which the Germans

View across No Man's Land at La Boutillerie from trenches held by the 21st Brigade, 7th Division. The German front line ran along the tree-line in the distance. It was on this sector that British and German troops met to bury the dead of the 7th Division's attack of 18–19 December. This photograph was taken after the 2nd Royal Scots Fusiliers had relieved the 2nd Wiltshires on 27 December 1914. *(Q 49102)*

Staff at work in the 7th Division's Post Office near Merville, 20 January 1915. It was establishments such as this which had to cope with the influx of letters, cards and parcels sent to members of the BEF each Christmas. *'The last parcel which arrived yesterday is a masterpiece. It has everything I want – paper and envelopes of which I had none, cold cure just when I have a rotten cough, pipes when Ringer has lost his . . . And the chocolate was a perfect Godsend. In fact chocolate is as welcome as anything, any amount of it, nice thick slabs . . . Everybody says what sensible parcels you make up and remark that you always send just what one wants.' (Pte Warwick Squire, 1/13th Londons) (Q 57350)*

Men of the 2nd Scots Guards in a barn on the road between Sailly-sur-la-Lys and Rue Pétillon, near Fleurbaix, December 1914. This building was used as a billet for the troops and venue for concerts. The 2nd Scots Guards were heavily involved in the Christmas Truce and an account of the events can be found in the letters of one of their officers, Lieutenant Sir Edward Hulse. His letters were privately published in 1916, and were extensively quoted from in *Christmas Truce*, by Malcolm Brown and Shirley Seaton. (*Q 57384*)

have of course as well as ourselves, and which it will be for good if they will realize that we have as well as for our men to realize in them.[13]

For support units, battalions at rest and those in reserve there was but a limited chance to become involved in the Christmas Truce. However, these troops were in a better position to provide themselves with additional food and comforts and some even managed to visit the front line to see if rumours of the truce were true:

Christmas was drawing near. My bearers were billeting in a farm just in the rear of 'Ploegsteert' church. On the Friday we decided to celebrate Xmas the best we could so staff segt Jones and myself went to a brewery and got 2 barrels of beer, not like the good old English beer. Of course our French conversation is not very fluent when it came to the asking how much it was, the woman shouted out something which we did not understand, Still we got the beer and paid.

We managed to get a piano from a house put it up in the loft of a farm and had a concert, drank to those at home, we spent a most enjoyable Xmas under the circumstances. Next morning we were paraded and our officer commanding, Colonel Prophet, handed us Princess Mary's gift with Xmas cards. Hearing from the troops in the trenches that they were having a truce, I went to the East-Lancs trenches and found the Germans and English troops burying the dead between the trenches. Cigarettes and cigars were exchanged. It was so exciting in this position to be above the trenches in daylight, at ordinary times it meant sudden death. (*David Lloyd-Burch, 10th Field Ambulance*)

Some troops were lucky enough to be billeted with local families, which provided them with a pleasant substitute for the Christmas they were missing at home:

We are now in billets in a farmhouse for 3 days rest. The family is very nice – girls from 16 to 4 and one little boy. After enjoying all the loving messages which your little Christmas tree brought us, I gave it to the little girl of 4, much to the delight of the family.[14] (*2/Lt Wilbert Spencer*)

Away from France and Flanders, a number of unlucky members of the BEF were spending an enforced Christmas in Germany as prisoners of war. One of these was Pte Thomas Rainbird, who had served with the 1st West Yorkshires (19th Brigade, 6th Division) until he was wounded and captured in late September 1914. When 25 December arrived Rainbird was in Doberitz prisoner-of-war camp. Here he found a distinct lack of rations, but the arrival of gifts from home helped give the prisoners a much needed lift on Christmas Day:

I must give an account of how we spent Xmas in camp. A good many of us received parcels from home containing cakes and puddings etc these

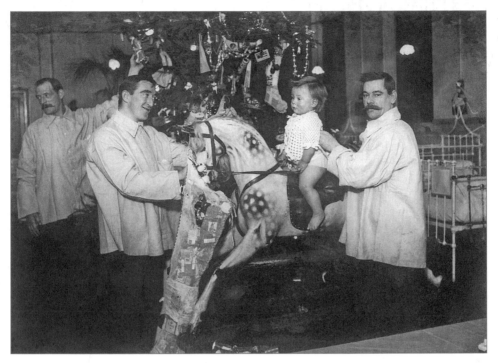

Wounded soldiers of the BEF give a child a ride on a rocking horse during a Christmas party at West Ham Hospital, December 1914. *(Q 53467)*

were heroically put on one side, until Xmas day, then each man who had anything took a chum who had not received anything and shared with him, so that every man had a little taste of the homeland, on Xmas Eve there was a heavy fall of snow, and Xmas morning we awoke to find a fine morning and three or four inches of snow on the ground. Then the fun started. The English and French formed sides against the Russians and then commenced a right battle royal. First the English rushed the Russian lines, with a terrible shout, the same shout doing more to dishearten the enemy than the actual snowballs. Charging and counter charging was the order all the morning.

In camps of a different kind, dotted all over the United Kingdom, many men of Kitchener's New Army were training and preparing to spend the festive season under canvas, in huts or billets in nearby towns. At Blackdown Camp, 3 miles from the rifle ranges at Bisley and

Men of the Army Service Corps at a camp in south-eastern England with their Princess Mary Gift tins, Christmas 1914. *'We each received a present from Princess Mary and a card from the King and Queen. The present consisted of a pipe and a tobacco tin, a packet of cigarettes and also of tobacco with a photograph of the Princess and a card.' (Rfm Richard Lintott, 1/5th Londons) (Q 53478)*

Pirbright, men of the 12th Rifle Brigade were granted a week's home leave for Christmas. However, as only one company could be away over Christmas proper, there was much interest as company commanders drew lots. Pte Harry Gore was in 'B' Company and ended up having to return from home leave on 23 December. But his disappointment was offset by the festive celebrations organised in camp:

> All the preparations were made for giving the men a good time. There was a prize for the best decorated hut. After church parade we sat down to a well prepared Christmas dinner, provided by the Company's officers. During the dinner the Colonel, with the Major, came round to wish us all a happy Christmas and we all returned the compliment.
>
> There was no drunkenness as on the Colonel's orders no liquor or spirits were allowed in the huts, although men could have a drink

at the canteen. The ruling was strictly enforced. After dinner there were football matches arranged and then later we sat down to a good tea. Cakes and other delicacies provided by the Officers wives. In the evening a concert was arranged, a party coming down from London to entertain us and was attended by the Officers, NCOs and men. Afterwards we had games in the huts until 'lights out.' Only one man came in from the canteen drunk, so drunk that we laid him on his bed and covered him over with his blankets and left him to sleep it off. He was the only one with a hangover in the morning.

At Colchester, Pte George Wilkinson of the 10th Royal Fusiliers was also looking forward to Christmas Day, having spent the previous night on duty in the Orderly Room, while his best mate, Pte Parnell, had been on Sergeants' Mess fatigue duty:

Christmas card produced by the 10th Royal Fusiliers in 1914. This unit was raised in the City of London and had the unofficial title 'The Stockbrokers'. Initially part of 18th (Eastern) Division, the battalion joined the 111th Brigade, 37th Division, in March 1915 and was sent to France during the summer of 1915. The design of the Christmas card includes St Paul's Cathedral and the Tower of London, two instantly recognisable London landmarks. (*Private collection*)

CHRISTMAS 1914   NEW YEAR 1915

When we came off duty we were told off as an Infantry Picquet and ordered to sleep fully dressed with our rifles by our sides in case of any disturbance occurring in the Garrison. In spite of our heavy boots we all slept well and were paraded at 7am on Christmas morning and dismissed, P and I went to Holy Communion at 7.15 and got back to brekker at 8 . . . At 10.45am we had a very smart Church Parade. At 1 o'clock Cookhouse sounded and we were formed up outside our houses to march to the double canteen for the Christmas spread provided by the Officers. The Sergt Maj waggishly remarked that there was no need to call the roll as 'Hevery man's ere' and as this caused much amusement he warmed up and gave the order 'Hevery man undo two buttons.' We had a jolly good feed, 500 of us sitting down together to roast beef, vegetables, turkey and sausage, Xmas pudding etc etc. Cheers were given for everybody and the whole thing passed off with more noise than I would have imagined possible. A concert was provided in the afternoon at which the Officers gave a touching sketch and a dance was arranged for the evening. P and I went out after tea and called in at the canteen on our return to see how the dance was getting on. With the exception of a few sergeants wives and two or three barmaids from the town and a programme seller from the Hippodrome there were no ladies, but the hall was full of chaps in heavy boots, some even with overcoats, dancing in couples round the room to the robust strains of our military band. P and I passed on.[15]

Boxing Day for the 10th Royal Fusiliers did not begin auspiciously as they made an early start on a route march headed by the battalion band. It began to rain almost at once and the men were quickly soaked to the skin. They spent the rest of the morning drying clothing and cleaning equipment. Luckily, the afternoon and evening were free and the troops made the most of their time:

In the evening I donned my cardigan jacket and Rene's scarf as my tunic was so wet and covered them with my overcoat and went down to the Hippodrome. 'B' Coy had the whole of the Stalls and two front rows in the circle. 'A' Coy managed to secure the boxes. P and I had seats against the big drum but were not deafened. Some time before the performance commenced numbers of chaps were dancing the Tango up and down the gangway and by the time the Orchestra appeared 'B' Coy in the circle had opened a bombardment on 'A' Coy with peashooters and a regular pandemonium reigned. I was wondering how it would all end but am glad to say it all passed off well without any trouble. One 'turn' walked off because a pea hit him just as he opened his mouth to sing. His retreat was ironically cheered. After this perfect order was kept while the 'turns' were on but in the interval rattles, hooters etc were very much in evidence.[16] (*Pte George Wilkinson*)

While those training at home were still able to enjoy some of the trappings of 'Civvy Street', others were embarking to garrison key points of Empire as the War Office recalled as many regular army units as possible for service with the BEF. On the whole, their place was taken by Territorial Force battalions such as the 2/4th Somerset Light Infantry, with whom Capt James Mackie was travelling to India on board the troopship SS *Saturnia*. On 24 December he wrote to his parents:

We hope to reach Port Said some time to-night so that when all of you at home are being awakened by the band we shall probably be entering Port Said. It seems very likely that the officers will be allowed to go ashore therefore in all probability we shall spend Christmas day on land although we shall have to come on board to eat our Christmas dinner. I saw the turkeys being drawn up from the hold and they looked awfully nice. After all if it were not for the heat we might say with the old song 'it's just like being at home' . . .

The Colonel is going to spend about £50 tomorrow in order to get the men a supply of Turkish delight, oranges and cigarettes: can you wonder that he is so popular . . .

We shall think of you all tonight when the smaller ones are hanging up their stockings and while we should like to be with you we feel awfully pleased that we are doing our little bit so that the rest of you may spend a very happy Christmas at home.

Two days later Mackie was sending home his account of Christmas Day in Egypt:

On Christmas morning when we awoke we were still in the same position where we stayed till 9.30. We had plenty to interest us for 10 huge liners came out of the canal and anchored quite close to us . . . Hundreds of boats came alongside with oranges, Turkish delight, etc making a very animated scene with the bright coloured clothes so typical of the East.

The officers were allowed to go ashore about 12 o'clock so we made for the Eastern Telegraph office and sent you a cable. This office is just opposite the place where we anchored. We felt quite at home as we steamed in for the first things we were able to read were Dewar's Whisky, Pear's Soap and Remington Typewriters.

My first impression of Port Said was that it was unfinished. With the exception of one street which is quite a good one, the houses seem unfinished or very dilapidated. The streets of the town itself are quite wide and the shops are excellent and as everyone can speak almost any language and will accept any kind of money we had no difficulty getting on. We visited the original Arab village which is very squalid and smells most unpleasantly. It is not safe to be anywhere except in the main streets after dark unless you are well armed.

In the evening those of us who were not on duty had a Christmas dinner at the Eastern Exchange Hotel and they did us splendidly. We had among other things the usual turkey, plum pudding and mince pies.

A few days later the SS *Saturnia* was heading down the Suez Canal and out into the Red Sea on its way to Bombay. Mackie commented on the scale of defences along the canal, the vital link between Britain and the resources of her Empire and Dominions.

The entry of Turkey into the war on the side of the Central Powers, on 29 October 1914, spread the war into the Middle East and opened up a new front against Russia in the Caucasus. Although Turkey would only become a significant combatant in 1915, the Entente's first move against the Ottoman Empire occurred on 6 November 1914, when Indian forces landed at Fao to secure the oil refineries there and at Abadan. These were of vital importance to the British given the Royal Navy's recent switch from coal-fired to oil-fuelled ships. The defences spotted by Capt Mackie along the Suez Canal were also a consequence of the Turkish entry into the war. Taking no chances, the British garrison in Egypt was swelled by the arrival of troops from Great Britain and India. With the 1/6th Lancashire Fusiliers at Abbas Hilma Barracks near Cairo was Pte Harold Henfrey:

I have spent a good Xmas and hope you have too. We had handkerchiefs and cigs sent from Todmorden and we all got 1 packet of Woodbines and 1 handkerchief, all Tod boys. I will now tell you what Bob Barker, Capt, gave us. We had to have our Xmas days food on Xmas Eve because our Company had to go on guard at Xmas Day and we had our dinner at 7 o'clock at night. First course pork with tatoes (potatoes!) and vegetables, 2nd course Potato Pie and vegetables, 3rd course Turkey and vegetables with cakes and as much beer, minerals, cigs, and twist as we wanted, and biscuits, then we all got a cig case and 5 piastres from Lord Rochdale, that was 1/d in English money. 5 piastres and we had a jolly, but it was rotten to be on guard at Xmas Day, but your Xmas cards and Nelly's card and all your cards cheered me up and made me think of the old old home while tears came in my eyes thinking of you at Tod with a Xmas dinner to sit down to. Mother I daresay you know we have gone in fresh barracks at Citadel at Cairo. It is a fort and I am on guard every other night so do not think anything about me if you do not get a letter every week for we have hardly time to write a letter, but we are settled down now and shall be able to write again every week now. Mother, am sending you a few postcards of round our barracks, a few of which we guard. Keep them and I will tell you all about them when I land back and I shall have lots to tell you about Egypt when I get back. The guards we have to do here are very dangerous and we have to keep our eyes open and be on the alert. We have 20 rounds in our rifle and if they do not halt on a challenge we have to shoot them down, and if we are found asleep on duty we are liable to be shot but I like to be on the watch and if any spies come knocking about I say shoot them. If a lad is soft on guard he will soon be game, for they are some of the strictest guards in the Army and we guard one place, the magazine, and there is 25 thousand million rounds of ammunition stored there so that lot would blow all Egypt up.[17]

By contrast, British military life in India was going on pretty much as it had done before the declaration of war on 4 August 1914. True, Indian and British units had left the country for foreign service, but for those remaining in the subcontinent the war seemed very distant. Capt Herbert Winn (2/5th Gurkhas), writing to his family on 29 December, provides an impression of the daily routine of a British officer in the Indian Army:

Gym 8–9am, drill 10–12, musketry 2–4. I generally go down to gym at 8 and do not return to my bungalow till about 5.30pm (I get my meals at the regimental mess). I then dress for dinner and have an hours read or so and then cycle down for dinner to the mess. Dinner is a very long and slow affair so that it is generally 9.30 before dinner is finished. I then cycle home to my bungalow and retire for the night.

Although Britain's 'jewel in the crown' remained seemingly unmoved by war, conflict quickly spread to other overseas possessions in the colonial empires of the opposing nations. In the Far East, the entry of Japan into the war against Germany on 23 August led to the quick occupation of the latter's Pacific island colonies, and troops from Australia and New Zealand took control of German New Guinea, the Bismarck Archipelago and Samoa during October. Only the German colony of Tsingtao in China provided any real resistance, holding out to a predominantly Japanese force until 7 November. Similarly in Africa, the German colony of Togoland quickly surrendered on 27 August. But in German South West Africa the initial capture of wireless transmitting stations on 10 August was not followed by a campaign to take the colony, as South African forces were tied down defeating a pro-German rebellion in their own country.

In East Africa, where troops of Indian Expeditionary Force 'B' attempted to capture the German coastal town of Tanga (2–5 November 1914), things were also quiet by December. The defeat of the 8,000-man force by 1,000 German Askaris of Colonel Paul von Lettow-Vorbeck's Schutztruppe came as a great shock to the British, who thought they would have to do little more than turn up to secure the town's surrender. A complete lack of surprise, lack of intelligence information, failure to make a preliminary reconnaissance, lack of cooperation between the Army and Royal Navy, the questionable ability of many of the infantry units involved and even a swarm of angry bees doomed the operation to failure. Maj Gen Arthur Aitken, commander of Expeditionary Force 'B', was ordered home and the forces in British East Africa were reorganised, with overall command going to Brig Gen Sir Richard Wapshare, who had commanded the 27th (Bangalore) Infantry Brigade at Tanga. For now the British remained on the defensive with little chance of receiving reinforcements in the short term. Of their new commander one of his staff officers is reported to have said: 'Wapshare is a kindly old gentleman, nervous, physically unfit and devoid of military knowledge; he is much too fond of physical comforts. He is known throughout Kenya as "Wappy". He is a heavy man fond of his food and dislikes exercise.'

These men, serving in East Africa, are seen receiving their Christmas (1914) gifts from Princess Mary. They arrived in March 1915. *(2006-07-19)*

This perhaps goes some way to explain the manner in which he spent Christmas in 1914:

Xmas Day. As we had the cook with us, O'Grady had arranged for dinners at the Norfolk Hotel. I went to office in the morning. In the afternoon they all went out shooting. I lent my rifle to Shepperd. He got a Grant and O'Grady a zebra. I stayed behind and sat for some time . . . and did some reading. Got a very gracious wire from the King, which I replied to. Also one from Lord K saying it was impossible to send more troops at present. Stewart again asked to be allowed to go. I've agreed and shall wire tomorrow. Had a nice quiet dinner with Shepperd, O'Grady, Dobbs, Hautrey, Powell and myself. Got back at eleven. We drank the health of our absent ones . . . I went to Church and Sacrament.

Sunday 27th Dec. O'Grady and I started yesterday . . . in a special carriage attached to a goods train. We got to [illegible] Station at 7pm . . . In the morning I started off at 6am on a trolley with the

Cpl Butler of the Bombay Section Volunteer Maxim Gun Company examines his Christmas 1914 gift of socks, which arrived at the unit's camp outside Nairobi on 1 March 1915. *(2006–07–19)*

Permanent Way Inspector. I shot 1 zebra, 1 gnu, 1 Grant's Gazelle, 1 [illegible] and 1 Tommy [Thomson's gazelle]. O'Grady went off walking, he got 2 Impala and nearly lost himself. He got back just in time for the train.

By contrast, in the German colony of Cameroon a far more warlike situation existed that first Christmas of the war. Here British columns made up of troops from the Nigerian and Gold Coast Regiments were moving against key German settlements and trading posts. This followed the capture of Duala, the main town, trading centre and wireless station on 28 September 1914. The country offered little in the way of roads and in parts was mountainous and heavily wooded, making it very suitable for defence. All supplies were carried by the troops and an army of African bearers. In a memorandum regarding an attack on Cameroon it was stated that German rule was very unpopular and that an invasion of the colony by British forces would be generally welcomed by the local population.[18] This however was not the experience of 2/Lt A.C.L.D. Lees (2nd Nigeria Regiment) when his troops first came into contact with local tribesmen whom he refers to as 'Pagans':

21 December 1914: Nothing in morning. Heard rumour highest peak had been abandoned, went all evening to try and find path up, attacked by Pagans. Pte Kuisa hit on head by stone. Retired, don't fancy Pagans in the dark.

Lees' diary records that both British and German troops were attacked in this manner when they came too close to some tribal villages. Apart from this he states that until Christmas the main activity was shooting at German sentries or anyone else who showed themselves. Then on Christmas Eve:

Had truce in afternoon to enable Christmas box to be sent to Sgt Taylor. Carriers forgot blankets, had to send them in evening. Saw Sgt Findley, Vincent and Evans at Posts A & B and gave box myself.

According to Lees' diary the truce held all the following day. Interestingly enough, war diaries for the various British columns and Nigerian infantry and artillery units do not mention any kind of truce. They simply state that the columns advanced on 25 December but met no opposition.[19]

On 30 December, all thoughts of Christmas receded as the 2nd Nigeria Regiment was given a rather distasteful duty:

Had orders to punish Pagans who had attacked me and wounded Kuisa. I do hate this sort of thing it is too much like murder. Ordered 7 men to attack at dawn. They started too soon about 2am (no-one here has a watch). Pagans offered stout resistance when men got back 3 had been hit by stones and they said 20 Pagans were killed. (*2/Lt Lees*)

At the same time two British columns were advancing on the important German trading post and fort at Dschang. From 21 December the troops marched over difficult terrain against an unseen enemy whose position was only given away when he opened fire. Typical of the fighting is that recorded on Boxing Day in a report by Lt Col Haywood, commanding the flanking column during the advance:

Small parties of the enemy with one or two Europeans were met and brushed aside at intervals until 2pm. Soon after crossing the R NKAM the road commenced to ascend a valley in the mountains. Scouting became more difficult owing to the dense bush encountered and the advance guard had to be reinforced to allow of picqueting the numerous hills. At 2pm when the main body was one mile from SANSCHU, I heard a terrific fusillade and machine gun fire in front.

A report reached me from Capt GIBB OC Advance Guard, that he was heavily attacked from the N and NW. I sent half the reserve to turn the E flank of the position and brought up the guns.

A body of the enemy on the NW who were annoying the column considerably were driven off after a few rounds of shrapnel.

Troops from a British column burn a native village in Cameroon to establish clear fields of fire against German Schutztruppe at Sava near Mora, December 1914. Although it was believed that German rule in the colony was so unpopular that a British invasion would be welcomed with open arms, such activity as the burning of villages did little to win over the native population to the British cause. Generally, the villagers wished to be left in peace and proved hostile to both British and German forces with whom they came into contact, as 2/Lt Lees discovered on 21 December 1914. *(Q 17205)*

It was difficult all this time to locate the machine gun and to find a position for my second gun to engage the enemy to the North. In the meanwhile our advance was checked. The turning movement took some time to develop and as a matter of fact, was not completed before dark.

A British naval 12-pounder gun outside the German fort at Dschang, Cameroon, shortly after the German garrison surrendered on 2 January 1915. The movement of this gun, along with the 2.95 inch mountain guns of No.1 Artillery battery, Nigeria Regiment, while difficult, gave a distinct advantage to the British columns advancing on Dschang. A short bombardment by the artillery caused the rapid surrender of the fort without the need for an infantry assault. *(Q 58001)*

About 5pm the machine gun was located and its harassing fire stopped by a few well directed rounds of shrapnel from Capt St Clair.

Next morning the turning movement being completed the column advanced and found the enemy had retired.[20]

Casualties in such clashes were light, this time being Colour Sgt J.J. Winter, who was killed along with two Nigerian soldiers. Seven soldiers and two bearers were wounded, the Germans losing four African soldiers killed and three wounded.

The Dschang expedition ended in success with the surrender of the fort and settlement on 2 January 1915 after a brief artillery bombardment. Col E.H. Gorges, commanding the Dschang column, summed up the effort his troops had undertaken:

The conduct and bearing of the native troops under fire has not escaped my notice. The men led by their British officers and NCOs have never hesitated to scout and advance through country the nature of which forced me to adopt a combination of bush and mountain warfare. The men are footsore and tired after three months continuous marching and fighting and the ranks have been depleted by casualties and sickness, but their spirit remains unbroken . . . In giving praise to the troops I must also mention the carriers with whom I have much sympathy; toiling with their burdens over mountain roads, through swamps and rivers and across unending sun-burnt plains, often suffering fatigue and exhaustion, yet patient, uncomplaining, cheerful and grateful even for an extra half ration. Without the African carrier our operations could not be undertaken.[21]

Christmas 1915

Another Christmas finds all the resources of the Empire still engaged in war, and I desire to convey on my own behalf and on behalf of the Queen a heartfelt Christmas greeting and our good wishes for the New Year to all who, on land and sea are upholding the honour of the British name. In the officers and men of My Navy, on which the security of the Empire depends, I repose in common with my subjects a trust that is absolute. On the officers and men of My armies whether now in France, in the East or in other fields, I rely with faith, confident that their valour and self-sacrifice will, under God's guidance, lead to victory and honourable peace. There are many of their comrades, alas, in hospital, and to these brave men also I desire with the Queen to express our deep gratitude and our earnest prayers for their recovery. Officers and men of the Navy and of the Army another year is drawing to a close as it began in toil and bloodshed and suffering, but I rejoice to know that the goal to which you are striving draws nearer to sight. May God bless you and all your undertakings.

The King's 1915 Christmas Message to his Troops

Failure by either side to win the war in 1914 led to reassessments of strategy and the realisation that the goal of decisive victory would be difficult to achieve. Increasingly the belligerents began planning for a long war, where the full resources of the competing nations needed to be harnessed for their war efforts. By early 1915, 110 Allied divisions faced 100 German divisions on the Western Front and, in the east, 83 Russian divisions faced 80 from the Central Powers.

For the BEF, 1915 was a year of disappointment. The Battle of Neuve Chapelle (10–13 March), although beginning encouragingly, was soon bedevilled by communication breakdowns and an inability to deliver reinforcements at critical moments. The pattern was repeated during the Battle of Loos, which began on 25 September in support of a major French offensive in the Champagne. Increasingly ill-considered attacks, poor handling of reserve, heavy casualties and little in the way of territorial gains paved the way for the replacement of Sir John French by Sir Douglas Haig as commander of the BEF in December. When fighting in the west petered out for the year in November, there had been 60,000 British, 250,000 French and 140,000 German casualties. The war had also taken on a nastier face through the use of gas, the Germans getting off the mark first with this new weapon on 22 April 1915 in the Ypres Salient and the British replying during the Battle of Loos.

For the front-line soldier, gas was just another problem to be faced in an increasingly mechanised war. However, as Christmas approached,

Troops revetting front-line trenches at Laventie to prevent collapse, December 1915. Similar conditions existed along many part of the front: *'The trenches were exceedingly wet and the weather very bad. Owing to there being no shelters from the weather in the front line, men suffered a good deal from exposure. Work chiefly consisted of laying floor boards in the trenches and repairing the sides where they had fallen in.'* (War Diary, 1/14th Londons) (Q 17402)

of more concern for the troops on both sides were the conditions in which they lived and fought as wet winter weather began turning heavily shelled areas into quagmires:

> All the trenches are in a deplorable condition. BARNTON RD – the main communication trench is only usable as far as the OLD BRITISH LINE (reserve line) and the front line is divided into various small 'Islands' – each inaccessible from the other except by night – when the method employed is to go over the parapet. Relieving is of course only possible at night and has to be done overland, the trenches being in many cases five feet deep in water. The weather is wet, which does not tend to make matters easier.[1] (*War diary, 21st Royal Fusiliers*)

Many of the hastily constructed British trenches lacked shelters for the men who inevitably suffered greatly from exposure to the rain, snow, water and mud. Even so, morale among the infantry remained high:

> We get a good many regiments of infantry pass here, on their way to and from the trenches. They don't half sing on their way back for a rest, and poor beggars, I don't wonder at it. They come out bedraggled and wet and smothered in mud from head to foot, but their spirit is simply wonderful. All laughing and cracking jokes, whistling and singing, they treat the whole thing as a joke. One would think they were on a picnic instead of a very bitter war.[2] (*Gnr Cecil Christopher, 47th Siege Battery, RGA*)

From early December, men of the BEF began to receive Christmas parcels from home. Although these often included home-made foods, the number of commercially produced edibles and 'comforts', including warm clothing and rubber boots, increased as department stores such as Harrods, Fortnum & Mason and Selfridges began to set up war comforts departments or produce catalogues of items suitable for sending to men at the front. Soon relatives were even able to purchase complete, pre-packaged, 'standard' boxes of food and 'comforts'. Harrods, for example, offered boxes for men serving on the Western Front, those in the Middle East and Dardanelles and even one for prisoners of war. But, wherever they came from, such extras were always

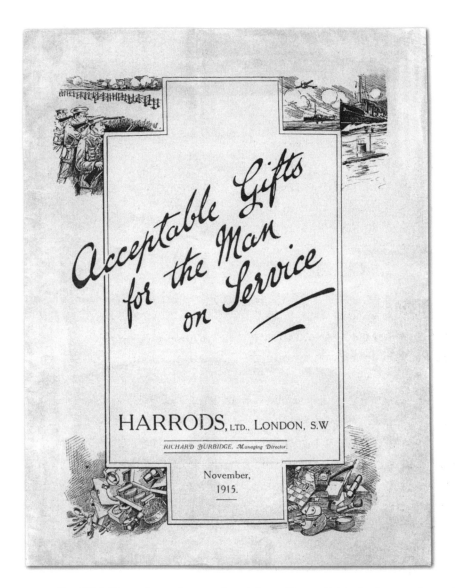

Front page of a 1915 Harrods catalogue advertising gifts available in the store's newly opened 'War Comforts Room'. The introduction to the catalogue reads: 'A Special Service for Soldiers and Sailors and Prisoners of War – Harrods have a large Section devoted solely to comforts for Soldiers and Sailors. This "War Comforts Room" is stocked with just those things which have proved to be most useful and acceptable to men on active service, or at home in training, and special attention has been paid to suitable gifts for Prisoners of War. Customers will find this Section a great convenience and Timesaver, as those goods which are ordinarily scattered over many departments are here to be seen in one room displayed side by side. The "War Comforts Room" is situated on the first floor above the Piano Department, and is well worth a visit of inspection.' *(Harrods Archive)*

welcome and at Christmas time especially the arrival of a parcel made the men think of happier days at home:

I must tell you I have just had my first Xmas pudding and a mince pie what one of our chaps as just had come so I daresay I am in front of you at home this year but I wish I wasent not half for as you must guess we would rather be at home for Xmas but still Dear Mother we must cheer up as best we can and make the best of a bad job for this as got to be done but we all hope to come back some day to you all if we are spared which I hope we shall be and I have had nother letter from the little boy at Northampton and he sent a packet of Woodbines in it so he a good boy is'ent he. So now Dear Mother I hope I shall get your parcel quite safe and I will let you know as soon as I get it and now Dear Mother I hope this will find you and all quite well as I am pleased to say I am at the present. So I will now conclude with my fondest Love and kisses to you and all for I remain your ever loving son Will xxxxxxxxxx for the girls.[3] (*Pte William Fall, 1st Entrenching Battalion, 2nd Canadian Division*)

Not all soldiers were fortunate enough to receive gifts from home, but their comrades would often share the contents of parcels and, on occasion, even went a step further:

Now Mother, I have a little favour to ask you, which I know will give you pleasure to carry out. It is this. We have a fellow here with us who hasn't a solitary relation in the world. That I know will be quite sufficient to tell you. We all seem to be getting parcels now except him, so I want you to send him a small parcel. It wont reach him till after Xmas, but I know the thoughts and wishes will be appreciated just the same. The fellows name is No. 35127 Gnr Overton, 47 Siege Battery.[4] (*Gnr Cecil Christopher*)

As for Christmas itself, the military authorities were united in their determination to prevent anything like the truce of the previous year from happening again. The Germans went so far as to declare that any of their soldiers found leaving the trenches to fraternise with the enemy could be shot for desertion. Within the BEF matters were not quite so draconian but firm instructions were given against any form of trucing with the enemy. Typical of these was a confidential memo from HQ, 140th Infantry Brigade, dated 19 December 1915:

The GOC directs me to remind you of the unauthorized truce which occurred on Christmas Day at one or two places in the line last year, and to impress upon you that nothing of the kind is allowed on the Divisional front this year.

The Artillery will maintain a slow gun fire on the enemy's trenches commencing at dawn, and every opportunity will as usual be taken to inflict casualties upon any of the enemy exposing themselves. (*War Diary 1/8th Londons*)

On receipt of such instructions, some battalion commanders stressed the matter by issuing their own directives:

With reference to the above, the Brigadier wishes you to give the strictest orders to all ranks on the subject, and any man attempting to communicate either by signal or word of mouth or by any other means is to be seriously punished. All snipers and machine guns are to be in readiness to fire on any German showing above the parapet. (*War Diary 1/8th Londons*)

Such concern was to a degree well placed as small-scale but prolonged fraternisation had taken place between British and German infantry at St Eloi in November and relations between opposing troops remained somewhat jovial on other sectors of the line:

4 December 1915: At 10am a good deal of excitement caused by Germans standing on their parapet and holding up their hands. A message was sent by them to the Regiment on our left suggesting that the British would find more comfort as prisoners than as soldiers. Our artillery and snipers promptly replied to the proposal. (*War Diary 1/4th Suffolks*).

Christmas card designed for the 6th Division by Pte W. Hunter (1/2nd Londons), 1915. *(E. Charick collection 81/35/1)* The verse inside the card reads:

> We're on our way / In the Berlin Express / The Bulldog – he's going it fine,
> You can see by his stride / And the Name on his side, / He's a Winner,
>   He'll break the Line.

Such behaviour continued in places despite growing feelings of bitterness towards the enemy. On the British side, the Germans' use of poison gas, bombing of British towns by Zeppelins and events such as the sinking of the liner *Lusitania* ensured there were fewer men inclined to have a friendly disposition towards the enemy than during the Christmas of 1914 and most troops in forward positions simply marked Christmas within their own unit:

We had just arranged this spread on Christmas day, when the Germans started 'strafing' us, but we still continued our feast and laughed at them. You may bet we enjoyed ourself to the full all day, as we did practically nothing all day and in the evening after we had all got into bed we had a few harmonized Carols which went down very well.[5] (*Gnr Ray Christopher, 47th Siege Battery, RGA*)

What military commanders wanted was for all their men to actively reject any peaceful overtures from the opposing lines, something that the 21st Division around Armentières appear to have carried out to the letter:

Xmas Day, comparatively quiet.

On the right the enemy appeared to want a Christmas truce as he was heard shouting 'We want peace'. What he got was five rounds rapid from six men.

The left sector report that the enemy showed the same disinclination to fraternize as we did. He kept up his sniping and sounds of jollification were conspicuous by their absence.[6]

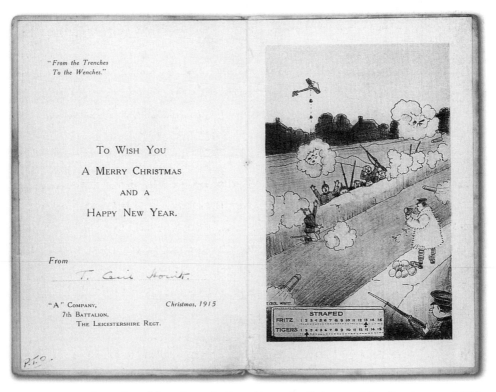

Christmas card produced by the 7th Battalion, the Leicestershire Regiment, 1915. (*A.E. Kaye collection 82/11/1*)

Some senior officers took personal steps to check that their troops were not engaged in any form of fraternisation. For example, on the front of the 1st Division the GOC, Maj Gen A. Holland, personally walked the whole length of the divisional front line and back along the reserve line on Christmas Day.

However, trucing did not entirely stop in 1915. At Laventie, close to where British and German troops had met the previous year, units of the Guards Division fraternised with their opponents:

> The German infantry (14th Prussians) came out of their trenches and walked towards our line. We did not fire on them as they had no equipment or arms of any sort. Some of our fellows went over to meet them. They shook hands and exchanged greetings, they also exchanged money and cigarettes etc. (*Pte William Tate, 2nd Coldstream Guards*)

The episode shocked the divisional commander, Maj Gen the Earl of Cavan, who quickly penned a report to XI Corps HQ:

> I much regret to report that in spite of special orders there was some communication held between the lines occupied by the Guards Division and the 13th Bavarian Reserve Regiment this morning.
>
> I have seen the Brigadiers concerned who were on the spot within 20 minutes of hearing of the episode and our men were back in the trenches within 30 to 40 minutes after first going out.
>
> I have ordered a full and searching enquiry to be made tomorrow as to how my implicit orders came to be disobeyed, which I will forward in due course.
>
> Large parties of unarmed Germans were the first to appear, but this is no excuse, and I regret the incident more than I can say.

On 26 December, 1st and 2nd Brigades held courts of inquiry into the incidents and the results were taken in person by Cavan to Gen Sir Richard Haking, commanding XIth Corps. On 29 December matters escalated with 1st Army calling for a report from XIth Corps as to the wording and transmission of orders issued to brigades, battalions, and

Christmas card produced by the HQ staff, 21st Divisional artillery, 1915. A humorous sketch of the HQ at work: *'Headquarters staff of the 21st Divisional Artillery, on active service, here in action, send you their Christmas Greetings from their "Little Grey Home in the West" (Front)'. (Lt Col O.M. Lanyon collection 92/19/1)*

companies forbidding fraternisation. On 4 January 1916, repercussions of the fraternisation hit the 1st Scots Guards with the arrest of their temporary commanding officer, Capt Miles Barne, and company commander, Capt Sir Iain Colquhoun. Their court martial began on 18 January, and representing the two officers as 'prisoners' friend' was Raymond Asquith, son of the British Prime Minister, who had met and become firm friends with Colquhoun while the latter was home on leave. The result of the hearing saw Barne acquitted and Colquhoun recommended for a reprimand. However, his punishment was remitted by Sir Douglas Haig because of Colquhoun's previous distinguished conduct in the field. Despite the flurry of investigation into the incident and prior warnings that severe action would be taken against individuals fraternising with the enemy, Barne and Colquhoun were the only two men to face censure over the event.

Behind the front line, troops were in a better position to celebrate Christmas, although enemy artillery fire and the usual round of fatigues and working parties intruded to some extent:

All through December 1915 we had been holding the line in the Neuve Chapelle Section but were in close support billets for Christmas, that meant we were responsible for supplying carrying parties to take up rations, water and anything else that was required by the men in the Front Line.

Although in support billets no kind of entertainment was laid on for us but of course we had to be always in readiness to answer a 'stand to' call if necessary, but we had extra rations and an attempt was made to make the best of it and as much relaxation as was allowed. The front line was about a mile away but in spite of that there were some civilians living around, mainly farm peasants and it was possible to get a meal of egg and chips, coffee, etc at some of the cottages of which some of us made use. (*Rfm Harry Gore, 12th Rifle Brigade*)

Most units reserved festive celebrations for the time closest to 25 December when they were billeted behind the lines at rest. This meant that troops could be found celebrating Christmas for three or four weeks around the actual date. Here the contents of parcels could be enjoyed, if they arrived on time, units organised Christmas dinners of numerous courses, sports competitions were run and concert parties could be visited.

In the village of Humbercamps the 13th Rifle Brigade, which came out of the line on 20 December, were one such unit:

It was Christmas Day at last. After an early parade we were dismissed for the day and while our cooks, with several self-appointed helpers, attended to such things as required cooking, the rest went to the village school which we had taken for the day and set up tables and prepared the stage. Never was there such a feast as we had that day. Never were

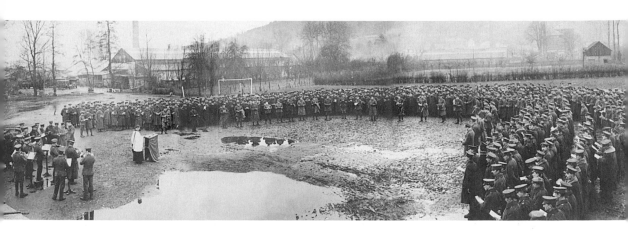

Christmas church parade at a base motor transport depot in France, 1915. *(HU 93158)*

there such turkeys, or ducks, or sausages, or puddings, or mince pies, or anything else that we consumed that Christmas. After a visit by the Colonel, the Adjutants, and our own Officers, all of whom wished us 'A Merry Christmas', and congratulated us on the well laden tables, we drank to 'The King' and thereafter the fun raged fast and furious. Mineral waters were provided in plenty for those of us who were teetotal and then, satisfied at last, we turned to the stage and prepared ourselves for the concert that was to follow. I have mentioned before that one of our number was an ex-music hall artist and there were others equally capable of helping to give a really good show, though we were by no means disposed to be critical. The village school mistress, a young French girl refugee from Lille, attended, perhaps fearing for the safety of the school property, but although enjoying ourselves to the full, we did no damage; she did not know any English and probably thought us more than a little mad, but as I say we heartily enjoyed ourselves and about 11pm we had to break up and return to our billets – if some had to be taken back, singing with all the power of their lungs, in a transport limber, there was, I think, some excuse for them. *(Rfm J.A. Johnston)*

Such activity, giving the men a little time out from the war, helped maintain morale even though many longed for the comforts and familiar surroundings of home:

Spent a very pleasant Xmas day, very different to the usual time – but a happy one nevertheless. We spent the time feasting and singing, some playing cards until 4am. Alf Gorton & F Dunn & self went to midnight mass – very nice – & it was such a beautiful evening to be out. What gave me most pleasure was thinking of home & picturing you all going round the usual Xmas routine.

Unfortunately our parcels did not arrive – in fact have not done so yet (*no body's*) – but expecting same any minute. However, we bought a tin of salmon for our Xmas dinner, was a change from stew & we got our issue of Tommies Plum Pudding – very good – 'but its not like being at home'. Whilst *enjoying* same I was picturing you round the bird, & other good things, the pudding & *sauce* & I could hear Ma saying to Mac 'I wonder what poor Arthur is having for his Xmas dinner?' Don't you worry, I was OK & have another good time in view when my parcels arrive. A chicken arrived for Tom nicely cooked & pies, and a parcel for us all from Miss Wilkins – so we went short of nothing. I had lots of post in the way of letters & cards many thanks to everybody. Tom's letter, Tot's card, another nice letter from Bamford, J & J, L Gregson, Marie K – about a dozen in all – very nice – got them hung up here.[7] (*Pte Arthur Burke, 20th Manchesters*)

In many of the villages in which troops were billeted a sizeable civilian population could still be found. The Christmas period lent itself to the fostering of good relations between the locals and members of the BEF. For example, at Souastre the 10th Royal Fusiliers gave a Christmas tree to the children of the village; the war diary of the HQ, 111th Infantry Brigade, also located in Souastre, records that the day was a great success and should go far to keep up the good feeling between the villagers and troops.[8] But sometimes the behaviour of the troops could become a little too boisterous, especially when alcohol had been flowing freely, as happened in one billet in Lillers:

We felt like we could relax at times like these and indeed we did. Quite a lot of us were billeted in an attic over a large Estaminet in the square and four of us planned to celebrate by having Christmas dinner at a café which offered quite good fare for four or five francs. We had no money but were expecting a pay on Christmas Eve. We were not idle when out on rest and on Christmas Eve my section were unloading timber at the railhead . . .

Well the unloading of the timber was ended and we were off duty. We still had not been paid and on enquiry we found that we would not be paid. Christmas dinner had been ordered. The section officer was on leave in England, whatever could be done about it? We eventually managed to borrow enough from the Company Sergeant Major who was a very decent and understanding man. We had our dinner and thoroughly enjoyed it. Christmas night was memorable to me. There were almost 30 men in our attic billet which was approached from a bedroom by a very rickety stairway. Most of the chaps were drunk, one or two of them so much so as to be suffering from DTs. Who cares? We were out of the line anyway. The section officer had sent us a huge box of Christmas crackers from home. They contained all sorts of miniature musical instruments. The result was a collection of weird noises from would be musicians.

It was alright till tempers became frayed and then I am afraid we became out of hand. Sgt Kayton and Cpl P Brown quarrelled. Kayton was stood near the head of the stairs and sticking his chin out, invited Phil to hit him. Phil caught him right on the point of the chin and down the stairs he went. Kayton did not seem to be hurt but he was quiet and gradually everyone also quietened down too and we got to sleep. The landlord of the Estaminet had a young married daughter with a newly born baby and we had been asked to be quiet. She came to the top of the stairs next morning, glared around and simply said 'Finish Christmas'. (*Cpl Bob Foulkes, 73rd Field Company, Royal Engineers*)

The year 1915 also witnessed the war spreading across southern Europe. Italy joined the Entente cause on 23 May, opening up a third front against the Central Powers. In October, British and French troops landed at the port of Salonika in neutral Greece in an attempt to keep Bulgaria out of the war and save their hard-pressed Serbian ally from inevitable defeat. However, of all the new fronts opening up,

Christmas card produced by the 7th Division in 1915, showing British infantrymen on their way to the trenches. The card was one of a number published by James Haworth & Brothers, London, during the war. *(Private collection)*

1915 will perhaps best be remembered for the landing of British, French and ANZAC (Australian and New Zealand Army Corps) troops on the Gallipoli peninsula on 25 April, in an attempt to knock the Ottoman Empire out of the war. The failure of British and French warships to force their way through the Dardanelles in March, in a bid to reach Constantinople, led to an escalation of the campaign, which had been planned as a purely naval operation. The initial landings at Cape Helles and Ari Burnu, soon to be known as Anzac Cove, achieved some success but were not quickly exploited, allowing the Turks to bring in reinforcements and prevent any meaningful advance. Trench warfare soon set in and stalemate as on the Western Front was the result.

Attacks across the confined spaces of the Gallipoli battlefields saw casualties mount rapidly. Conditions deteriorated during the summer with dysentery being rife among the troops. Some of those evacuated wounded or sick were lucky enough to be put on board hospital ships bound for Britain rather than Egypt. This gave the imperial motherland its first glimpse of the ANZACs, who were making such a name for themselves at Gallipoli:

Just a line to let you know that I am out of the hospital, and am on six weeks' furlough, and am having a splendid time. The weather over here is pretty rotten – rain or snow every day – but we are enjoying ourselves immensely. The people here are treating us very well; in fact, all England is open to us. I will tell you how I spent my Xmas – from the time I got up in the morning. I had a wash, then breakfast, went down to the reading room for a read and a smoke, down stairs to the barber's for a shave, and then had my boots cleaned, after which we started out to have Xmas dinner with Sir George Reid at the Hotel Cecil (in the Strand), one of the largest and best hotels in London. And I tell you it was a dinner, too. There were about 900 Australians and New Zealanders present. You may guess what it was like when I tell you that any civilian that wished to be present had to pay 10/6. Sir George Reid and several other noted men gave speeches. Well, after we had had dinner and came out into the Strand again, several of us were accosted by a lady we did not know. She asked us if we would be good enough to go and spend the afternoon and have tea with her. Of course, we accepted the invitation, and were placed in taxis and driven off. We did not know where we were going, or whose house we were going to, but we were happy. However, it turned out alright, for it was Lady Wolsley's place we went to, where we had a right royal time. We had just escaped from there when we were caught again, and put into taxis and whirled off to spend the night and next day with a Mr and Mrs Lauder, parents of a great musician who has just returned from a tour in Australia. So you can see we did not want for much. I am going to Scotland on Wednesday for the New Year, where, they tell me, the people are even better than what they are in England, so we must be in for a good time. I am going to stay with a Mrs Grey, in Edinburgh, while there. I think I will also go to Glasgow for a few days.[9] (*Pte Frank Scholes, 14th Battalion, AIF*)

Back at Gallipoli, in August, 25,000 men were landed at Suvla Bay in an attempt to capture the all-important high ground overlooking the Dardanelles by outflanking the main Turkish defences, but once again initial successes were not exploited and the last hope of strategic success in the campaign vanished. By late November, winter weather had begun to set in and gales, thunderstorms, torrential rain and blizzards made life in the trenches and dugouts a misery:

21 December 1915: A thunderstorm and heavy rain last night did more damage than a month's shelling. In many places fire and communication trenches were impassable and everywhere mud rendered movement slow and difficult. (*War Diary, HQ, Royal Naval Division*)

The coming of Christmas at least gave the hard-pressed troops something pleasant to focus on:

Sketch by Lt Col Dan Mason, sent home to his family from Gallipoli and bearing the motto, If you think we're down 'earted we ain't. (*97/18/1*)

At a camp outside Salonika, men of the 12th Argyll & Sutherland Highlanders listen to their commanding officer's speech on New Year's Day 1916. It was at similar parades that the King's Christmas message was read out to troops in all theatres of war. *(Q 31612)*

One night just before Christmas I was on duty in the Signal Office and the Commander was busy in his office which had now been partitioned off when he called out to me 'Freeman can you cook a Turkey?' I thought he was getting on at me on account of my performances with the Dixie on various occasions, so I said 'Yes Sir, I think so.' 'Well' he said 'we got one for you.' I was too much astonished to say anything for a moment and then thanked him as well as I was able for his kindness. He had, he told me ordered two to be sent from Tenedos and was going to give us one of them. There was great rejoicing in the camp when I told the others the great news! In the place of Haywood, who had returned to his battery, we had a new cook named Watson, he was a farmer before he joined up and knew how to deal with the insides of turkeys in the proper manner, he was quite pleased to take over the job from beginning to end, which suited the rest of us very well. We had

had many discussions regarding our Christmas fare but never in our wildest flights of fancy did we think of a turkey – although I suppose it would be difficult to find a more appropriate place in which to eat the bird than Helles. I had a real home made Christmas pudding in a china basin, which had miraculously arrived unbroken in the post, but we decided to keep this for the new year as supplies were issuing tinned pudding. Altogether things looked very promising. Christmas Eve we were all very merry and bright and feeling very fit. Peattie and I made quite an 'arty' Christmas card for the Commander and Johnstone in which we all signed our names as a sort of memento of the time we had been together and Watson, who was proud of his skill in the making of pastry, insisted on manufacturing a large apple turnover on a plate for presentation to the Commander on Christmas day!

I was up at 6 o'clock on Christmas morning and after a wash outside in the moonlight, walked down to 'W' Beach to early service. The morning was dead calm and almost undisturbed by firing of any sort. A little way out to sea lay the two hospital ships, each with a line

The Royal Naval Division HQ Signals Office, Gallipoli, 1915. This is the 'summer' quarters which the staff, including Corporal Stanley Freeman, were forced to vacate in December 1915 for more solidly built accommodation due to the worsening weather conditions. *(Q 61081)*

of green lamps running from stem to stern, looking as if they had on their Christmas decorations. Away to the right Achi – the still unconquered – was just a grey outline, an outline we knew by heart. Dotted about in all directions twinkled little points of light which might have been the reflection of the stars in still water – camp fires getting ready for breakfast . . .

The service was held in a marquee behind the ordnance stores. The pews were planks supported on biscuit boxes and the altar was of packing cases covered in front by a slip of cloth and lit by two candles. Two dim oil lamps hanging from the centre of the tent did their best. The simple words of the service went home to most of us I think. I was glad I went . . .

We also had a limited supply of French wine which had been swapped for superfluous jam. Again I say pity the poor soldiers at Gallipoli! The afternoon was quietly spent as you might imagine. After tea we made up a big fire, lit plenty of candles and enjoyed ourselves. We played cards, Peatties band played various selections as long as those who were not musical, shall we say, would let them; and we talked of many things. By 10.30pm most of us were in bed. I was on duty at the office at 1am again but we had got so used to getting up in the middle of the night that we did not worry about it . . .

At 1.30am an enterprising Taube came over in the moonlight and dropped a bomb about 50 yards from the redoubt, we found parts of it in the morning . . . and all was quiet except for a few rounds from Asia whistling overhead at intervals, destined for 'W' Beach.

So passed Christmas Day 1915; we had no idea that there was the slightest probability of leaving the Peninsula for good in just over a fortnight's time. (*Cpl Stanley Freeman, Royal Naval Division Signals Company*)

The evacuation of the peninsula proved to be the most successful part of the whole Gallipoli operation. Between 18 and 20 December troops were withdrawn from Suvla Bay and Anzac Cove. The position at Cape Helles was retained slightly longer, but on the night of 8–9 January 1916, the last troops embarked. Only a handful of casualties were reported during

Cookhouse of the 1/11th Londons at Sidi Bishr, Egypt, January 1916. This battalion had fought at Gallipoli and had been evacuated from the peninsula in December 1915. *(Q 49002)*

An officer carves the Christmas turkey in the Mess of the 26th Divisional Supply Train, Salonika, 25 December 1915. *(Q 31571)*

Men of the 26th Divisional Supply Train, ASC, lining up for their Christmas dinner, 25 December 1915. *'Certain hardy venturers had done some bargaining with local shepherds and peasants for sheep and geese, but the geese were not all that they promised to be when sold, and the sheep were rather like overgrown rabbits when stripped of their skin. But it was undoubtedly a noble Christmas and will be long remembered.' (Maj Frank Debenham, 7th Ox & Bucks Light Infantry) (Q 31573)*

the operation, confounding those who estimated that up to half the force would be lost in any withdrawal. On board the troopship *Knight of the Garter* Capt Herbert Winn (2/5th Gurkhas) summed up the feeling of many in a letter home written on 23 December:

Am rolling about at present in the above-mentioned boat. Everybody is bored to tears and feeling ill from over-eating and over-sleeping. We are not allowed on deck during the day for fear a submarine sees us and discovers there are troops on board. Not that anyone would have wanted to stroll about today as a driving rain is beating along the deck. Altogether things are not, just at the present moment, wearing a very pleasant aspect. Yet at the back of everybody's mind there is the soothing thought 'we have left behind those confounded trenches' and this compensates for all.

As the Gallipoli campaign was in its final few months the 10th (Irish) Division and French 156th Division were withdrawn from that operation and sent to Salonika, where they landed between 5 and 10 October 1915. By the end of November these troops, along with the French 17th (Colonial) Division, were in the mountains of southern Serbia facing the

Officers versus other ranks football match being played by members of the 26th Divisional Supply Train near their camp, just outside the city of Salonika, Christmas Day, 1915. Among other units playing football that Christmas was the 8th Duke of Cornwall's Light Infantry. Their inter-company matches had the following results: 'A' Company 3 : 1 'D' Company; 'B' Company 2 : 1 'C' Company. Final: 'B' Company 4 : 0 'A' Company. *(Q 31574)*

Bulgarian 2nd Army. Here they were hit by the same appalling winter weather that affected those still at Gallipoli. This led to 23 officers and 1,663 men being evacuated. They were suffering from frostbite and exposure even before the Bulgarian offensive began on 7 December. Five days later all remaining British and French troops were back on Greek soil and moving towards the relative safety of Salonika. On 14 December, the decision was taken to fortify and hold Salonika rather than withdraw troops from the Balkans. By 20 December, when the last of the 10th Division returned to the city, they found the place beginning its transformation into a huge military encampment. On the British side the 22nd, 26th, 27th and 28th Divisions were in the process of arriving, signalling a major commitment to this new theatre of war.

Macedonia is a land of climatic extremes with hot, blistering summers, at that time accompanied by the arrival of malaria-carrying mosquitoes, which at times caused more casualties than enemy action. In contrast the winters could be very harsh with heavy rain, blizzards and the bone-chilling Vardar wind, which blew for days on end on to the plains of northern Greece:

We were served out with woolly skin coats that made us look like a polar expedition. We had to scramble marches over the mountains where the snow lay feet thick. Rum was served out and extra blankets and anti-frostbite ointment for the feet and when you dressed in the morning boots and puttees were frozen stiff and waterbottles solid.[10]
(*Pte Reg Bailey, 7th Royal Berkshires*)

For men of the British Salonika Force (BSF), that first Christmas in Macedonia would be spent either at the base area around Salonika or in the foothills north of the city constructing a 70-mile-long chain of defences to protect the vital port from seizure by the Bulgarians. This work lasted five months and proved particularly difficult over the winter for the troops living in tents in the hills and ravines due to a combination of the weather conditions, rocky nature of the ground on which the defences were constructed and the lack of tools and engineering supplies. For Christmas, each unit tried to mark the holiday as best it could:

Xmas Day, 1915, was a red letter day. It was not much of a 'holiday', for urgent works were carried out as usual for half the day. However, we got the afternoon and evening off. What made it a day to be remembered was that on that day we got the first mail we had had for five weeks – since leaving France – and also our first issue of fresh meat and bread: bully and biscuits having been our fare all the time. Half a rum issue also marked the day. Although Salonika was only seven miles away, great difficulty was experienced in getting up supplies, owing to the shocking roads and fearful weather.[11] (*Capt Melville Rattray, 107th Field Company, RE*)

Down at the base camp matters were a little more comfortable:

We really had a very decent time for Christmas considering conditions; we are fortunate in having one or two very good cooks in our party – we built a special oven and had roast beef and chickens, with potatoes and bacon; puddings made on the spot and a really excellent cake – almonds, tangerines, biscuits, chestnuts to roast on a brazier, beer and lemonade according to taste etc etc. We had a game of football in the morning on quite a respectable bit of ground.[12] (*Pte Richard Stratton, 15 Sanitation Section, RAMC*)

At some of the newly established depots and hospitals, concerts were performed for the troops in large stores tents and marquees temporarily fitted out for the occasion:

At half past seven we went to a concert in a store tent with biscuit boxes as seats. It wasn't a great success as there was no piano. Our star turn was a couple of Highlanders one of whom piped while the other danced a sword dance. There was a large opposition party outside which hadn't been able to come in and it howled lustily while our songs were on. The funniest item was a huge fat labour sergeant who started about four keys too high who, after a piercing shriek, said 'I can't sing' and rushed away. It was a lovely night outside with clear moonlight. All over the plain for miles were rows and rows of lit up tents and

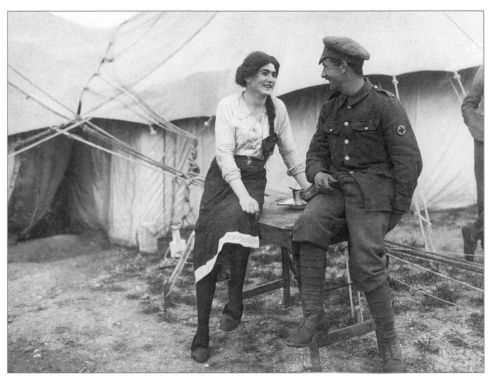

Frank Kenchington (right), writer of the pantomime *Dick Whittington*, first performed by members of the 85th Field Ambulance on Christmas night 1915. With Kenchington is Corporal Edward Dillon who played Alice, the heroine of the piece. As well as writing the pantomime, Kenchington also played the role of chief villain, Count Maconochie. *(Q 54731)*

twinkling camp fires, and one could hear the cheers and shouting in the distance all around.[13] (*2/Lt Eric de Normann, ASC Main Supply Depot*)

Among the productions was a version of the pantomime *Dick Whittington*, performed by members of the 85th Field Ambulance. With its villains Count Maconochie and Sir Joseph Paxton, named after brands of tinned meat and vegetable stew and jam that were staple rations of British troops during the First World War, this show became such a hit that it toured to all units of the 28th Division. Following years would see the players of the 85th Field Ambulance perform the equally popular *Aladdin in Macedonia* (1916) and *Bluebeard* (1917), again penned by Frank Kenchington to reflect army life in the Balkans.

The 5th Connaught Rangers on parade before Mass at 0845 hrs on Christmas morning. This photograph was taken by the battalion commander, Lt Col Henry Jourdain, who wrote of the Christmas Day: '*Xmas Day on the sandy flats near Salonika, with the prospect of as good a time that was possible, but still away from home and all the comforts that were possible there . . . The whole country was covered with frost and looked quite white at 7am. Afterwards the sun came out. I distributed cigarettes and some parcels of comforts and gave the men an issue of rum and some beer. They behaved very quietly and well and there was never anything that could be classed as undue hilarity.*' (Q 55144)

Such entertainments were very important in maintaining morale, for Macedonia was very much a foreign land with its barren countryside and often difficult climate. Even the city of Salonika was closer to an eastern rather than a European city with its minarets and cosmopolitan population of Turks, Bulgars, Greek and Spanish Jews. That the BSF found itself at the end of a long maritime supply route also caused problems as the Mediterranean quickly became a happy hunting ground for German and Austro-Hungarian U-boats operating from bases in the Adriatic. The sinking of shipping not only affected the levels of rations, equipment and ammunition available but also made the evacuation of sick and wounded to hospitals on Malta, in Egypt and Britain an increasing problem. In addition the flow of letters and parcels from home was also interrupted, something that was especially felt by the troops at Christmas time:

> There is a rumour going about that the mail-boat has been torpedoed and all the Christmas parcels gone to Davy Jones. The millions of Christmas puddings and tobacco and stuff we were to have had from all over the world have dwindled down to a couple of square inches of pudding from the Daily News . . . we are now pushed up in the hills miles from anywhere and we all feel very, very fed up and far from home.[14] (*Pte Jack Webster, 10th Devons*)

Further afield, increasing commitments were being made by the British Empire in Mesopotamia. Not content with securing the oil fields in the south, forces under Gen Sir John Nixon, spurred on by the India Office which had overall responsibility for the campaign, began to advance along the River Tigris towards Baghdad. Easy initial victories against mostly locally raised Turkish forces led to huge overconfidence on the part of the senior commanders. Maj Gen Charles Townshend, leading the 6th (Poona) Division, supported by a flotilla of river gunboats and transports that became known as 'Townshend's Regatta', accomplished an astonishing advance, relying more on bluff and the incompetence and disarray of enemy forces than sound strategy and tactics. At the Battle of Ctesiphon (22–25 November 1915) the lack of troops, artillery and an

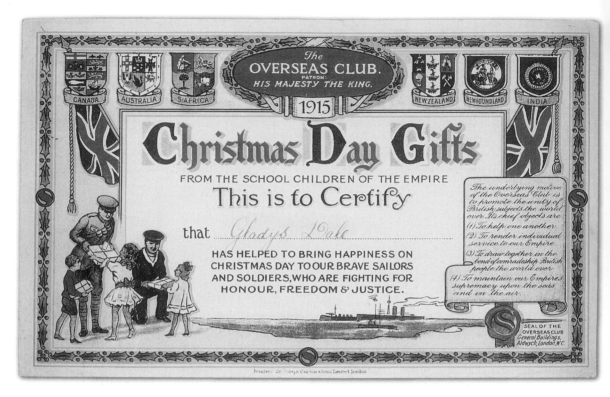

Certificate given to schoolchildren across the British Empire by the Overseas Club as a reward for sending a Christmas parcel to a serving soldier or sailor, 1915. *(MISC 192/2846)*

overextended line of supply finally caught up with Townshend. Unable to break the Turks he retreated to Kut-al-Amara where from 7 December his forces were besieged. During the first month of the siege the Turks, not having to worry about the activity of other British forces in the region, tried to gain an early victory:

> Christmas Eve was the best scrap I ever wish to see. It was on a cold and frosty morning (really it was) that the Turks opened fire on our rotten, mud walled, so called Fort . . . and it was soon evident that their intention was to batter down the walls and all that therein was, and so be able to enfilade our front line and thus walk into Kut.
>
> As our guns had strict orders not to engage artillery we lay low, and damned glad we were to do so in that inferno . . .

Quite early, about 7am the fire became very accurate and as we went out to try the telephone both the Maj and myself were knocked down bustle over hairpins by a shell, but were not touched, only warmed. This was followed by another which burst in the door of the Mess dugout, busting my six bottles of whisky which I had only bought the day before from the Oxfords for Christmas Day (Gott Straffe Turkey) . . .

About 11am the shell fire intensified and there was precious little left of the mud walls from the Sirmoor Bastion to the East Bastion and the 119th Infantry had been badly shaken mostly from being buried under tons of mud and 'Bhussa' mixed. The state of this regiment's nerves was reported to the O.C. Fort, but apparently no steps were taken to bring up fresh troops . . .

As we reached the barricade each man found his own place beside the Oxfords and opened up a rapid fire at the sea of yellow jackets and long bayonets on the broken walls. Our bombers were hurling grenades into the brown as hard as they could light the fuses – 4 machine guns were spitting out a cross fire of death at a range of from 30 to 80 yards. The Howitzers and 104th Battery's shells were crumpling outside – the din was appalling.

After using up my own, the wheelers and Capt. Dorling's revolver ammunition, an Oxford's brains were blown out alongside me, so I was able to get to work with his rifle.

In the 30 minutes we were there about 30 Oxfords and 103rd were killed, mostly shot through the head . . . The many wounded were quickly cleared out as our elbow room was very cramped.

At the end of half an hour the Turks were seen to waver, turn and run – while our men, Oxfords, 103rd and volunteers leaped forward on the battered walls, yelling and firing like demons . . .

This finished the show, not a shot could be heard anywhere in the deadly calm that ensued. The whole place was a mass of smoke, ammunition boxes, unexploded bombs, dead and wounded, broken rifles, bits of bodies and chunks of brain! . . .

By jove, there were many dry throats after this, and how I cursed the Turkish gunners for straffing my whisky, however the Maj had some!!

Officers of the 48th Pioneers halt for a meal near Mount Amara in the typically featureless landscape of Mesopotamia, 1915. *(Q 92691)*

After this attack had failed all was very quiet except for a few stray shells falling about, but as the afternoon wore on, we saw large numbers of infantry coming up into the trenches so all preparations were made for another attack. Barricades were strengthened, barbed wire 'spiders' thrown over the wall . . .

At 5.20pm everyone was ready, with the men to man the barricade sitting in the trench just behind it.

The night fell dark, with a full moon just showing through cloud and haze, and it was very cold sitting there waiting for eventualities.

At about 7pm the enemy suddenly sprang from their trenches and rushed at the bastion yelling 'Allah! Allah!' their advance being headed by lines of bombers (we gave them Allah alright and sent many to

Allahlujah!) Immediately everyone sprang to their posts and as soon as the Subadar of the 103rd blew his whistle to show that they were clear of wall B we opened fire at the dim shadows in the gaps of the wall to our front: we were greatly helped by 'Very Lights' which showed the enemy up well.

Men started to fall very fast, Br. Palmer was the first, Wheeler Gunner Manning next, both shot between the eyes . . . the din was terrific; 'Bhussa' bales and loose timber began to burn, a volley of bombs literally wiped out the 103rd in gallery A . . .

The Oxfords and our men were falling fast . . . and the smoke of the shells drifting slowly over us added to the general bonfire effect.

British troops in the trenches in Mesopotamia preparing to use a Haddick cooker. This apparatus used 3–4 gallons of oil per day and would cook any sort of food for a large number of men. *(Q 92643)*

After about an hour's hard firing . . . our numbers at the barricade were getting rather low . . . It was now that a bomb, or it may have been several, burst right among us and seemed to clean out all the defenders . . .

By the time I had got up and felt myself there was no one left, so the Major and I decided to make for the second line trenches, but finding the trench three yards in the rear of us full of able bodied men, he shouted out that there were enough to hold on, and back we jumped. The Major would not fall out to get his wound dressed and at the time I did not know he was hit in the shoulder, as his face was covered with blood. Davern with his maimed hand also would not fall out and now did yeoman work stuffing ammunition into our pockets which enabled us to keep up a heavy fire . . .

At 11.30pm we were relieved by the 48th Pioneers, and thankful we were to go back to the 2nd line, as all were pretty well cooked after four hours solid firing in the dark. While the Major went off to get orders I took the men that remained, to the trenches by our guns and we all started to oil our rifles and many odd ones we had brought away, and had not been there long when Gunner Skinner appeared with a 'decktchie' of tea and hunks of bread spread with salmon, where he got it from Gawd only knows, but it was some supper I reckon.

We sat there wishing each other a Happy Christmas under rather novel conditions, and just to cap up the Sergt Major and myself split my flask of whisky . . .

The Norfolk Regt relieved the Pioneers at 3am and there was a certain amount of firing, but the Turks had taken their punishment early and had no stuffing left in their attacks.

While waiting to get the wounded out I fell asleep where I sat, and no longer heard the snores and moans of our exhausted and wounded men. (*Capt Keith Freeland, Royal Garrison Artillery*)

While the Kut garrison were engaged in fierce fighting, other troops in Mesopotamia were having a more restful Christmas. Men of the 1/5th The Queens (Royal West Surreys) were on outpost duty along the River Euphrates:

Christmas card produced by Indian Expeditionary Force 'D', Mesopotamia, 1915. *(Private collection)*

Xmas day K. Post. Reveille at 6.30, breakfast at 7.30. Tea and milk, bread and butter, salmon. Our tent is in lying picquet and not allowed to leave post so unable to go to Church at all. Dull with cold wind and air full of dust. Received message from King wishing the troops in Mespa a Happy Xmas that the goal for which we are fighting for was in sight, also message from O.C. 5th Queens wishing all at K Post a Happy Xmas. Stuffing dates all day. Xmas dinner cold boiled chicken and beef, hot turnips only vegetable obtainable and Xmas pudding no currants etc were to be had dates were added in their place not so bad considering everything. Tea – tinned peaches, bread and butter and milked tea, turned in about 9.45. Came off picquet 5 o'clock. *(Pte Henry White)*

Page from Harrods General Catalogue of 1915, advertising a range of chocolate and sweets suitable for sending as gifts to soldiers serving overseas. *(Harrods Archive)*

The next round of major operations would have to await the New Year when sufficient troops were gathered for the attempted relief of Townshend's force at Kut.

While numerous units of the Indian Army prepared to embark for Mesopotamia, those battalions sent out from Britain the previous year were well settled in numerous garrisons across the subcontinent and British-controlled islands in the Indian Ocean. One such unit was the 2/4th Somerset Light Infantry, who were based at Port Blair in the Andaman Islands. By December they had sat out the malarial season, although numbers of men now began to pick up ringworm which, while not too serious, was annoying and uncomfortable. The battalion's officers were also enjoying new cuisine, among which was parrot pie, the main ingredient for which were shot by the officers. As mailboats from India were none too regular the battalion's main recreation was cricket, either within the battalion or against the local Gymkhana. Strangely enough, Christmas Eve found the Somersets on alert for a possible German raid to free Indian nationalist prisoners from the large penal colony on the islands, something the Indian military authorities had been expecting since August:

John was at the wireless station, Andrew at Ross and I was sleeping in a tent on the barrack square and when I turned out at 4am feeling very sleepy I went to the signallers and got them to signal Christmas greetings to John at the wireless station and in a few minutes a reply was flashed back wishing the same to me. Then we repeated the message to Andrew on Ross. This is the first time we have ever wished each other a merry Xmas by means of heliograph. Neither John or I will be able to eat our Xmas dinner tonight for we shall both sleep out under the stars. John will be in charge of a picket at the wireless station and I shall have one at Corbyns Cove about three miles out, and I don't expect there will be much sleep for either of us. For about a week now we have been standing to arms at 4pm remaining out till daybreak, but it will not last much longer for we were to be attacked on Christmas night, when the enemy no doubt thought we should all be feasting. However they will not catch us napping this time if they come, but it is very unlikely that they will get here for we are surrounded by a huge fleet of warships. The mails came in yesterday and brought your letters for Nov 18th but we have had none of the letters between Oct 20th and Nov 18th . . . I am going up to barracks in a few minutes to see that the men's Christmas dinner is alright. The money for it has been provided by Willis, but beside this the people of Bath have very kindly sent out about £50 for the same purpose so the men will not do at all badly. We have got turkeys for them locally and green vegetables and oranges came down from Rangoon yesterday. Owing to the trouble no man is allowed more than two pints of beer but I don't think this restriction is very necessary for there have only been about three cases of drunkenness since the Regiment came to Port Blair.[15]
(*Capt James Mackie*)

If the war had not been going well for Britain in Europe or the Middle East during 1915, her forces were gaining victories in Africa. The most vital of these came in February, when a determined Turkish attack on the Suez Canal was defeated. However, the forces on hand were not strong enough to pursue the defeated enemy across the Sinai Desert, leaving a potential Turkish threat to Egypt. In German South West Africa, South African forces took a lead in forcing the surrender of the colony on 9 July 1915. This freed troops for offensive operations in German East Africa, although it would be 1916 before sufficient manpower was available to really challenge von Lettow-Vorbeck's Schutztruppe. Until that time British forces were primarily engaged in trying to prevent German raids against such strategic targets as railways. The one major Allied success in East Africa was the sinking, by naval gunfire, of the German light cruiser SMS *Konigsberg* in the Rufuji River delta (11 June 1915). Progress was more tangible in Cameroon, where British columns, largely composed of African troops, had, by the close of the year, brought the German defenders close to defeat. These campaigns in the colonies could be tough in the extreme in terms of climate, disease, poor rations and lack of comforts available in most other theatres of war. Even some of the old Africa hands, officers who had been attached to their units since before the outbreak of war, found things tough going:

This is a curious life if you come to think of it, here are most of us who have been out here some time richer than we have ever been before yet all in rags and likely to be living off rice and maize in a few days time. A cheery prospect for Xmas and of course nothing to drink.

It does make one grouse a bit after having kept fit for so long to run the chance of getting run down for want of a little arrangement.

The price for what one can buy locally are simply enormous like native tobacco and the worst imaginable cigarettes especially made for native trade and sold at 1/- a 100 in peace time are now being sold for a mark a piece.

We are getting on quite satisfactorily with our advance south but it is slow work and to average 5 miles a day is very good . . .

David is in great form. He is on this column and is a jolly good soldier. A bit quieter now that we are teetotallers under compulsion. From the papers it seems if England was a dull place now and I gather one is looked upon as unpatriotic if one orders champagne. What ho for the chance, I think we deserve it.[16] (*Capt Eric Barclay, 2nd Nigeria Regiment*)

Christmas 1916

I send you my sailors and soldiers, hearty good wishes for Christmas and the New Year. My grateful thoughts are ever with you for victories gained, for hardships endured, and for your unfailing cheeriness. Another Christmas has come round, and we are still at war, but the Empire, confident in you, remains determined to win. May God bless you and protect you.

At this Christmastide the Queen and I are thinking more than ever of the sick and wounded among my sailors and soldiers. From our hearts we wish them strength to bear their sufferings, speedy restoration to health, a peaceful Christmas and many happier years to come.

The King's Christmas Message to his Troops, 1916

By the third Christmas of the war the scale of the conflict, especially on the Western Front, had grown again. A strategy of attrition had taken hold and the ability of each nation to sustain the demands of total war was put to the test. This was the year of those defining battles of the war, Verdun and the Somme. The latter operation was one of a number of co-ordinated Allied efforts across the Western, Eastern, Italian and Salonika Fronts in an attempt to greatly weaken the Central Powers by preventing Germany, and to a lesser extent Austria-Hungary, from concentrating their forces. The Somme battle, which was to have included a major contribution by French, became a primarily British operation once the scale of the German effort at Verdun was realised. The battle would witness the blooding of a large part of 'Kitchener's Army' of volunteers. By the time Haig called off operations on 19 November, the Somme had claimed 419,654 British and Dominion casualties, 204,253 Frenchmen and 600,000 Germans. The first day of the battle, 1 July 1916, was the

Damaged British trenches near Ploegsteert Wood in the Ypres Salient, January 1917. This photograph clearly shows the poor state that trenches could be reduced to during the winter months. *(Q 4664)*

bloodiest day ever for the British Army, with some 57,470 casualties. It also witnessed the first major operation by the ANZACs on the Western Front, namely the taking of Pozières (25 July–5 August). There were also innovations such as the first use of tanks (15 September), improvements in infantry-artillery cooperation and a growth of tactical knowledge across the vastly expanded British Army.

When Haig closed down the offensive in November, it was primarily due to the deteriorating state of the ground over which his troops would have to advance. As Christmas approached an additional month of bad weather had taken its effect on the trenches:

The 33rd Division had taken over the front line that had been held by the French about the beginning of December and the 16th was holding a part of the line near Maricourt and Clery. The condition of the communication trenches, support and front line trenches were terrible, very few dugouts and general conditions as bad as they could be. The dead, mainly French, were still lying about in No Man's Land . . .

After a few days rest we were ordered in again in the same sector. This was the period of Christmas and we were in from the 23rd until 26th December. Once again strict orders were issued to the effect that there was to be no fraternization with the enemy and indeed such was the condition of the ground between us – 'No Man's Land' – that it was not possible or desirable. (*Rfm Harry Gore, 16th King's Royal Rifle Corps*)

A Canadian gunner writes the message 'I am the Hun's Father Christmas' on the side of his 9.2 inch Howitzer, Somme, November 1916. *'For about ten days our gunners enjoyed themselves knocking Jerries' prized possessions to bits, while our infantry carried out lots of raids to supplement the artillery's efforts. Fritz of course did not like it, so naturally he retaliated. We did not like it either because the ground was frozen solid at least three feet thick and his whiz-bangs, instead of just going into the mud and going off "pop" and doing nothing else, ricocheted and went off "bang" and threw bits about; so a few of us got hurt.'* (2/Lt F.M. Hahn, 9th North Staffords) (CO 1024)

British officers sliding about on ice-covered shell holes on the battlefield of Beaumont Hamel, December 1916. (*Q 1686*)

The 14th Argyll and Sutherland Highlanders found similar problems in trenches north of Bouchavesnes on 26 December. Here, some communication trenches were filled by waist-deep mud leading to most movement being undertaken across the open:

> During the whole spell of 5 days rain fell nearly every day which made any special work on the trenches absolutely impossible. Owing to the fact that this part of the line is a salient the bringing up of rations was very hard. Even over the top the going is very slow and parties were being constantly held up by someone sticking in the mud. Dugouts were very scarce and any that there were were old and damp. There is little to report during this spell as little more than the mere occupation of the trenches was possible. (*Battalion War Diary*)

Knowing that their coming spell in the line was liable to allow little in the way of Christmas cheer, the Highlanders celebrated early:

On the 24th we had our Christmas dinner which was held in one of the huts and it was quite a decent affair. Of course we had no tables or chairs and we had just to sit on the earth (no floors) and eat the various courses out of the top of our mess-tins, the bottom portion being used to hold a couple of pints of awful French beer, but the latter was better than nothing to drink at all. We didn't bother to wash out our tins between the courses . . . which were soup, mince (no potatoes), figs, pineapple, plum pudding. The usual concert followed given by members of the company. Concert parties from home don't venture this length. We enjoyed it immensely and knew it was the last time before we had gone through a bad time, so we made the most of it.[1] (*Pte Robert Lawson, 14th Argyll & Sutherland Highlanders*)

The generally poor conditions at the front not only ended active operations on any large scale but ushered in the by now familiar struggle to maintain trenches and dugouts. As both sides were engaged in this work and having to cope with daily life in the mud and rain, an attitude of 'live and let live' could be found along numerous sectors of the line:

Before going any further I'll tell you how things are round here – you will hardly believe it, though you may have heard of such cases before but it's *absolutely true*. Fritz and us up here are on absolutely speaking terms – he comes over and exchanges cigs etc – it got so frequent it had to be stopped and even after our order to quit, two of our boys got 28 days for going out and meeting him half way for a chat. There's never a rifle or machine gun shot fired by either side for many days, although we got orders to fire we knew it was hopeless to do so – so we didn't. You see both of us are only holding shell holes which meant us going over the top for 150 yards or so and had we fired on him he would have returned the compliment so that was the understanding between us.[2] (*Pte Arthur Patrick Burke, 20th Manchesters*)

At Le Touret in the La Bassée sector, two companies of the 9th North Staffordshires were sampling life on a quiet part of the line after taking part in three months' fighting on the Somme. In 'A' Company's Officers' Mess

British troops purchasing geese for their Christmas dinner, Bailleul, December 1916. The relative closeness to the front of towns still occupied by civilians gave troops an excellent chance to purchase many extras for their Christmas celebrations. *'Spent all yesterday and today preparing to give the Bn a Xmas dinner tomorrow. Went into Amiens by lorry-hopping and brought back sacks of apples and vegetables so that with a special issue of port we can do something.' (Capt James Wyatt, 2/4th Gloucesters) (Q 1629)*

the big task of Christmas Eve was to secure some whisky. Following a tip-off from officers of a Royal Fusilier battalion a case of scotch was procured from an army canteen in Bethune. By way of a thank you, 2/Lt F.M. Hahn was dispatched with a few bottles to the Fusiliers. After partaking of a few glasses a number of officers decided to go out into No Man's Land to see what the Germans were up to and to sing them a few carols. Hahn was invited to accompany the group:

We crossed No Man's Land and, parading in front of Fritz's wire, began to sing Christmas carols to them.

Fritz responded by standing up behind their lines and singing their carols, in German, to us. Our North Stafford patrol, hearing the

British troops eating their Christmas dinner in a shell hole near Beaumont Hamel, 25 December 1916. *'We have been up the trenches for a week and I have had no time to drop a line to anyone. Well I am pleased to say I am quite well after it all. We are back again for a short rest, I don't know for how long and we have been busy cleaning ourselves up all the time. We were in a state, plastered all over with mud, everything smothered up. Well old chap, what sort of a Christmas did you have, very quiet all round I suppose wasn't it. We spent Christmas in the Front Line. At least Christmas Day and it was a bit noisy.' (Rifleman Jim Watts, 6th KRRC)* (Q 1631)

cheerful noise, came and joined us, and we passed along the German front, singing and exchanging friendly badinage with them. There was no hatred about it! A few hours ago we had been blasting each other to Hades, we killed them and they killed us; but that was part of the game; we did not hate each other; we both knew that, and for Christmas, for that day only, the Spirit of Christianity prevailed.

Goodwill continued to prevail when Hahn returned to his battalion's lines. Here he noticed lights showing in a farm building to the rear of their position:

I knew only too well what it meant. Our company was having a Christmas Eve dinner of roast duck . . . Fritz however, did not even fire a rifle shot at that farm building while the party was on. In normal conditions it would have been too good an opportunity for his artillery; but he knew that if he did we would spoil his Christmas for him; and the spirit of Christmas prevailed and the company enjoyed a splendid Christmas Eve dinner of roast duck. I am afraid, however, that the supplies of French beer for Christmas Day were somewhat depleted . . .

Such attitudes did not prevail everywhere as there were always those who zealously followed to the letter orders warning against attempts to fraternise with the enemy:

21–26/12/16: In line again received parcel from home containing roast turkey and sausages. Invited all gun team to dinner and had a royal feed. Sent share to Bill Percy in support (including parsons nose). Fritz fairly quiet. Fritz showed himself during the day and invited us into no-mans-land to meet half way. Maj Gordon saw them and ordered two snipers to fire on them, which they did. The Batn called him a dirty dog and so he was. It was an unBritish act, as the 9th KLR were doing work in our trenches and encouraged Fritz by shouting and waving. He did not fire, in fact he appeared to be unarmed. (*Pte Walter Hoskyn, 5th King's (Liverpool) Regiment*)

Where there was no overt contact with the enemy, troops in the line simply passed Christmas as quietly as they could and took advantage of any small comforts they could find:

'D' Coy held the front line until early Christmas morning and the Lewis Gun team found a small dugout which we could use when off duty and turn about. It was very quiet and there was no sniping or gunfire during that period but a sharp lookout was constantly kept. We were relieved from the front line about an hour before 'Stand To' back to support lines about a hundred yards behind the front line. Conditions were a little better but not much . . .

Men from one of the Black Watch battalions of the 15th (Scottish) Division, celebrating the arrival of the New Year in a hutted camp at Henencourt, 1 January 1917. *(Q 4642)*

Soon after 'Stand Down' the Commanding Officer . . . came to wish us all a Happy Christmas and expressed sorrow that he could not drink our health because his bottle of whisky had been mislaid. Afterwards it was found that some of our Platoon had found it and drunk it. It was surprising the CO never smelt it but if he guessed what had happened to his whisky he was sporting enough not to notice or say anything about it. He was a very fine man and a very good officer.

Christmas Day passed off very quietly but the next morning we had to carry two of the Lewis Gun Team down to the First Aid Post suffering from Trench Feet and they could not walk. We were allowed to go over the top but were under orders to come back by the trenches, but not liking the conditions in the trenches we disobeyed the order. Fortunately, we were not spotted by the CO, officers or German snipers. *(Rfm Harry Gore)*

Troops coming out of the line just before Christmas hoped to spend a relatively comfortable time in huts or billets. However, the shortage of furniture and other comforts meant that any camp not permanently occupied was liable to be stripped of anything useful, leaving a rather desolate appearance to weary men returning from the front:

Friday. Dec. 22nd
Up and away at 9am and marched through mud to Aveluy reaching there at 12 noon. We found the camp which we left ten days ago fairly comfortable, an absolute wilderness. All the chairs, tables, beds etc have been pinched for some other camp. So we set to and started a pinching campaign. We visited other surrounding camps and within as hour had enough to make the place presentable again. I fear the people in the camps were all out on working parties for the day! They will have a shock on their return! (*Capt James Wyatt, 2/4th Gloucesters*)

British press chauffeurs drink the King's health at their Christmas dinner at Rollencourt Chateau, 25 December 1916. (*Q 1632*)

Signallers early on Christmas Day received messages of action at the front, which were probably formulated to prevent any feelings of goodwill from spreading across No Man's Land. But apart from these brief reports there was little to spoil festivities:

Very heavy strafe by our arty in Armentieres area. 2nd Anzacs made a raid and found enemy trenches deserted and were not able to bring back any identifications of any kind . . . I was on duty at 6.30. Took off Xmas message from Commander in chief wishing all ranks a happy Xmas and victorious New Year. At 1pm we sat down to a nice Xmas dinner of roast pork, potato, cabbage, stuffing, apple sauce, Xmas pudding, custard, stewed fruits (apricots, peaches, pears), biscuits,

A sign in Fonquevillers advertising the 5th Division's concert party, the 'Whizz Bangs', December 1916. There was always a great demand for such shows and the performers always made a special effort at Christmas time with musical reviews and topical version of pantomimes. *'In the evening took the Coy into Senlis to see the 51st (Highland) Divisional "Balmorals" or pierrots! It is really a wonderfully good show. The first show I have been into for six months too. The men all enjoyed it thoroughly.'* (Capt James Wyatt, 2/4th Gloucesters) (Q 1633)

oranges, apples, nuts, several boxes of cigars, good cigs, beer for those who drunk it, citron (lemonade) and Grenadine (made from cherries) and soda water for the TTs. The aft was devoted to practising songs for the concert in the evening. 4.30 tea consisting of jellies, custard, stewed fruits as above, mince pies, and the rest as above. Concert commenced 6 o'ck and I had to give 5 songs. Some of the time was given to dancing and as we had some Belgian people in who had helped us with the preparations of the food they enjoyed it immensely. I made a few attempts and got on tolerably well towards learning. We packed up at 11.30 after which I went on duty all night. (*Sapper David Doe, 51st Signal Company, RE*)

Where possible the inclusion of civilians in festivities appears to have been widespread from the number of entries in letters, diaries and memoirs. As well as being a way to ease the burden the war had placed on them, if only for a couple of days, the presence of French and Belgian civilians provided some continuity with peacetime Christmases through the inclusion of the elderly, women and children; all reminders of the people the soldiers had left at home. So, the chance to have Christmas dinner in a family environment was too good a chance to miss:

When I awoke this morning my first thoughts were of the dear little girlies and I fancied I could see them running down to get their little stockings and bringing them up and turning them out on the bed. Of course they hung them up, didn't they. I was with you too about midday and could see you all at dinner and imagined what all your thoughts would be. 'I wonder what kind of Xmas dinner Mowbray is having'. Well dear, I can say I had the best dinner today I've had in the Army. We had roast pork, potatoes and cabbage, Fig pudding, Jam roll, Xmas pudding and Jelly. Of course that was of our own procuring and not Army rations. The Old Frenchman and his wife at the Farmstead sat down with us and there was 17 of us all told. She cooked the joint and vegetables for us and one of our fellows made the puddings. Of course the Xmas puddings were yours and one of the other fellows' wives. The fellows wished 'Good Luck' to the makers

British soldiers having a snowball fight with French children near Rollencourt Chateau, British Press HQ, February 1917. *(Q 4689)*

of them so I pass it on to you and hope you will enjoy their wishes. We have not yet had our 'Daily News' pudding, but I think we shall be getting them in a day or so. It has not been a very nice day today – very windy and some rain, somewhat like last Xmas was if I remember aright . . . I have been very temperate, did have two *small* drops of port – there is only myself and one other young fellow who doesn't take anything. He only has port and rum. If I drank beer I could have had plenty, but I am not sorry.[3] (*Pte Mowbray Meades, 2nd Middlesex*)

For soldiers from Australia and New Zealand, Christmas 1916 was their first on the Western Front. Though a good number had already experienced terrible winter conditions at Gallipoli the previous year, for new drafts the difference to home was marked, although the army did its best to give men a break from the conflict:

I shall tell you how I spent Christmas; I guess very differently to anybody out in dear Australia. (Oh, lovely land of sunshine.) Well, we went to bed as soon as we could last night, as we were very tired, having been going from 7 o'clock in the morning till 8 at night, first with a load of coal and then with a very big load of rations, which we took to a spot over twenty miles away. We went to bed thinking, well, we had a chance of not being pulled out too early, as they said we were doing two days' work in one, so as to have Christmas as free as possible. Imagine our feelings when at 3 o'clock this morning we were

A typical Nissen hut camp on the Western Front. This one is at Fricourt on the Somme, December 1916. Although such camps on former battlefields could look bleak, they did offer a degree of warmth and comfort much appreciated by men coming out of the line. *'Christmas 1916 was passed in huts at Bertrancourt and a fairly decent Xmas feed was enjoyed by all. Roast Beef and potatoes and plum pudding were included in the menu and beer was issued as a health to the season. The surroundings could not have been better, everyone being reminded by the former good cheer that although so far away from home they had not forgotten what took place in civilian life.'* (L/Cpl Doanal Dobney, 22nd Manchesters) (Q 1711)

Christmas card produced by the Royal Naval Division in 1916, making light of trench conditions on the Somme that winter and showing the advantage of having a naval background! The card was printed in Paris by Gr. Devambez, 63 Passage des Panoramas. *(MISC 209/3047)*

called up, to go out, and have breakfast after we had finished the job. It was pouring rain, dark, and as cold as charity. I thought, 'A merry Xmas, and no mistake.' We were up to our ankles in mud, and the engine was in a terrible starting humour. Well, the job was on coal, and we got finished and were back for breakfast at 11 o'clock, but it was a good breakfast. After the rain ceased and things had a more pleasant aspect I got to work on washing some clothes, which I had wanted to do for about five weeks . . . Well, I got to my washing and did it all, and then I sewed four of my brass buttons which had come off on to my Australian overcoat, and after that it was our great Christmas tea. It was in two of the huts, and electric light had been put on from the workshop. Long tables were up each side, and were decorated with fancy paper flags and Chinese lanterns, all got from the Expeditionary Force canteens. They looked really splendid. All of us sat down, and the N.C.O.s waited on us, and they did it well. I may say the whole thing was run and paid for by our own canteen. On the tables were apples, walnuts, dates, cake and bread. The first round was ham and turkey, roast beef, green peas (tinned) and cabbage, and as much as you could eat, and I have never tasted better turkey. For those who wanted it, there was as much French beer as they liked. As you can guess, a good many were having a hard job to balance theirs, and it set their tongues in great working order. After the meat came Christmas pudding and sauce. I can tell you it is the best meal I have had since I left home. Then we had some songs. There is a Sgt England here, and he has a most glorious voice. I fancy he was on the stage. He sang, 'A Perfect Day,' and sang it beautifully. I gave 'Three for Jack', and when I started I hadn't the faintest idea what the words were, as it had never crossed my mind since goodness knows when, but I got through it without a bloomer, and we had no piano. Some others sang, drank and did otherwise, and all got a good hearing. The whole thing passed off splendidly, so our Christmas Day had a very bad beginning but a splendid ending. I forgot to tell you that every man got a bon-bon, and each had a paper cap inside. We all put them on, and you can't imagine the funny sight it was. I saved mine and got a little flag and a tinsel flower off the decorations, also a lantern, and I am going to send them to you to keep as souvenirs of a Christmas spent with the British armies at the front, and at the very hottest front. By jove, our guns were sending over some Christmas greetings to Fritz last night, and are doing so now intermittently.[4] (*Driver Alan Gillespie, 2nd Ammunition Sub-Park Transport, AIF*)

For a lucky few the Christmas period coincided with their turn for home leave. The chance to return home was eagerly taken even if the journey to the Channel ports could take rather longer than anticipated:

Monday, Dec. 25th

Arrived at Candas at 12.30am. There we had to walk to the other station. On the way we all, about 300 of us, stopped at a Y.M.C.A. for some hot coffee. We went on to the other station from which the train should have started at 2.30am. The train however apparently went wrong somewhere; anyway we were told to go back to the Y.M.C.A. and return at 8.30am. We returned to the Y.M.C.A. and were all asleep when at 4.30am, a porter came to tell us that we were to go on by a special train coming up the line from Doullens. Just then I suddenly found out that I had left a rug in the last train. So with the idea that I had plenty of time I went off to the other station, found that the train had gone out, presumably with my rug, and returned as quickly as possible, just in time to see the special leave train disappearing up the line! Never mind, there is an ordinary train in the morning to Longpré and from there you can catch a Calais train. I lay down in the Station Master's hut, and was soon asleep. I woke at 8am Xmas Day!!! The train left at 8.30am. I spent some hours in Longpré and got some food. Thence by slow train through Abbeville, Etaples and Boulogne to Calais. I spent the night in a hut prepared for officers on leave.

Tuesday, Dec. 26th

Awake at 7.30am and to breakfast at the Gare Maritime. There I found many I had left in the leave train I had missed the previous night. It seems the train got in so late, that they lost the leave boat in the afternoon. The boat left at 10am and we were all aboard by 9.45am.

Artwork from inside a Christmas card produced by the 16th (Irish) Division in 1916, showing two soldiers of a ration party carrying Christmas dinner to the front line. *(MISC 145/2276)*

We had a very smooth crossing and reached Folkestone at 12 noon. The train went very slowly and only reached Victoria at 2.30pm. I caught the 3.35pm from Euston, and reached Northampton at 5.20pm after a journey of 48 hours. And so home once more. (*Capt James Wyatt*)

The Britain to which Capt Wyatt returned had undergone a number of changes. Conscription had been introduced for all men aged between 18 and 45 years of age under a Military Service Bill of 25 January 1916. The following month, to increase government access to funds for the increasingly expensive war effort, a National Savings scheme was introduced. In May, daylight saving was brought in with the introduction of British summer time. Through this measure it was hoped to increase production in factories and munitions works. The year had also brought armed conflict to the British Isles when, on 24 April 1916, members of the Irish Republican Brotherhood seized the General Post Office in Dublin and declared an Irish Republic. British forces put down the uprising within a week as it had lacked popular support, with fewer than 2,000 people taking part. However, the execution of Irish rebel leaders won much sympathy for the republican cause, forcing the British government to maintain a sizeable garrison in Ireland for the remainder

Artwork from inside a Christmas card produced by the XV Army Corps in 1916, showing the activity of both front-line and support troops of the Corps. *(Lt Col O.M. Lanyon collection 92/19/1)*

of the war and leading to civil war and ultimately independence in 1922. But, by Christmas 1916, the situation on the British home front appeared calm, Ireland was quiet, the Royal Navy's victory at the Battle of Jutland (31 May–1 June) seemed to underline British dominance of the seas and military training camps were full of men being prepared to take their places in the front line for what were hoped to be the decisive battles of the coming year.

At No. 2 Balloon School of Instruction, Lydd, new members of the Royal Flying Corps (RFC) were looking forward to what would probably be their last Christmas before overseas service:

I hope you will have a nice time at Xmas. As for myself it will be my own fault if I don't as the week's programme in Lydd is one continuous

Christmas decorations inside the Sergeants' Mess at Harrowby Camp, Lincolnshire, 28 December 1916. *'Once again to the Dining Hall. What a transformation! The place had been cleared out, tables rearranged to make one big table, holly and decorations had converted the place into a fairyland . . . cotton wool did duty for snow and altogether it was very fine.'* (2 ACM Frank Haylett, No. 2 Balloon School of Instruction, RFC Lydd) (8505-05)

round of entertainments, bun fights, picture shows, sermons, lectures, dinners etc etc. I am sure we shall all be ill. We have a terrific feed in the camp on Xmas Day. Turkeys, fowls, puddings galore and everything everybody can think of – nothing to pay – all refreshments on – beer, cigarettes and so on. I tell you this is some Corps. We all went to church this morning and I must say I was proud to belong to the RFC, compared to the RGA, we fairly set the town agog. The drill and parade went off splendidly and numbers of the Lydd folk stood by and looked on almost amazed. The preacher gave a very good sermon and choked off the RGA men for coughing continuously in church – a very severe rebuke which they wont forget in a hurry . . . I have hardly done a stroke of work since I came back to camp – everything is at a standstill, all the heads having cleared off for a week or more . . . I went for a joy ride on my own motorbike on Friday to Ashford and spent nearly

Certificate given to schoolchildren across the British Empire by the Overseas Club as a reward for sending a Christmas parcel to a serving soldier or sailor, 1916. (*MISC 192/2846*)

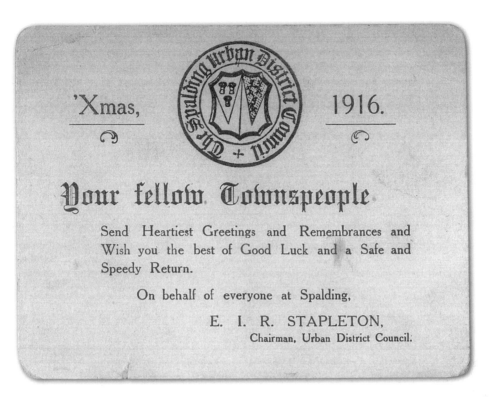

'Xmas,   1916.

The Spalding Urban District Council

Your fellow Townspeople

Send Heartiest Greetings and Remembrances and Wish you the best of Good Luck and a Safe and Speedy Return.

On behalf of everyone at Spalding,

E. I. R. STAPLETON,
Chairman, Urban District Council.

A Christmas card sent by Spalding Urban District Council to local men serving with the armed forces. The card possibly accompanied 'comforts' parcels sent by the town to its servicemen. *(MISC 157/2432)*

all day there – no one missed me and I never said a word to anybody. The camp is a picnic just now if it were not for the mud one could not possibly grumble. Have just done a 24 hours guard and came off at 9 o/c this morning. This is quite good because I shall not now get any more during the Xmas – my only fear was that I should be on Xmas or Boxing Day.[5] (*2 ACM Frank Haylett, RFC*)

In India too all appeared calm with little to threaten the smooth running of the Raj. For many troops, Christmas on the subcontinent appeared to usher in another round of ceremonials and social events:

This week we have spent a good deal of time rehearsing ceremonial as 100 of my men have to take part in the Viceroy's State entry into Calcutta tomorrow. They will be commanded by one of my subalterns as I have to attend at Government House for the reception. He is going to stay a few days in Calcutta and will then come out to Barrackpore for a fortnight. I have to attend all sorts of functions during the next week or two. On Saturday night I have to dine at the United Services Club, as the Viceroy is going to be present there: and on Boxing day there is a party at Government House Calcutta in his honour. When he comes out here there is sure to be a dinner party and a garden party which we shall have to attend.

The men are going to have a jolly good time this Christmas: the people here are going to give them a first class dinner and then they are to have sports in the afternoon and a good tea. I am very glad indeed that so much is going to be done for them for they have worked well and deserve to be looked after this Christmas time, especially as the people round here are making fortunes out of the war. Fortt and I have been invited out to dinner on Christmas day by some very nice people and I think we shall have a jolly good time.[6] (*Capt James Mackie, 2/4th Somerset Light Infantry*)

Festivities did not end with the feast of six courses provided for the Somersets by the English community of Barrackpore:

After dinner there were sports for us all which were awfully good fun. Some were mounted and some were on foot but all the events were amusing: perhaps the one which caused most fun was the bullock cart race. A bullock cart was provided for each competitor drawn by two bullocks and each man had to drive his lady partner to a certain point – you would have roared to see our frantic efforts to make the bullocks trot and when they did trot we could not make them go straight.

One of the mounted races consisted of riding your pony at a gallop past a lady who threw you a ball. You had to catch the ball and then gallop on and put it into a bucket. I went in for it but was unable to catch the ball.[7] (*Capt James Mackie*)

In Mesopotamia, troops from India found themselves far removed from the style of peacetime soldiering that still persisted in their homeland.

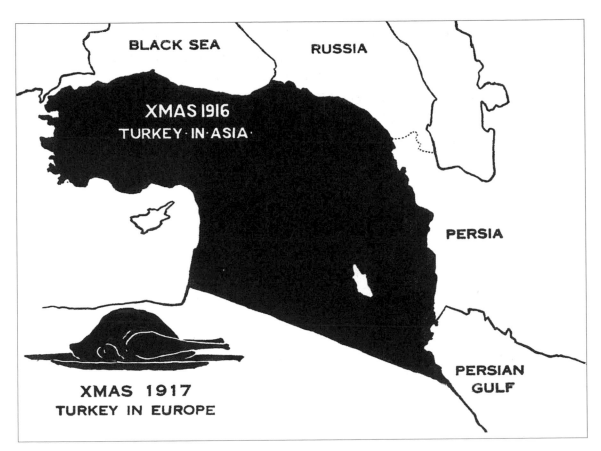

Artwork from the inside of a Christmas card produced by the 1/5th The Queens (Royal West Surreys) in Mesopotamia in 1916. *(Private collection)*

The early months of 1916 witnessed increasingly desperate attempts to relieve Townshend's besieged garrison at Kut-al-Amara. Forces under Maj Gen Sir Fenton Aylmer and later Lt Gen Sir George Gorringe attempted to batter their way through strong entrenched Turkish positions along the Tigris. Although the Turks lost some ground, the relief force suffered heavy casualties as it fought its way over open ground in the face of heavy machine-gun and rifle fire. This and the inability to move reinforcements quickly to the front sealed the fate of Kut, which surrendered on 29 April. Turkish success here, coming just four months after the final evacuations at Gallipoli, was a severe blow to British prestige and many feared it would trigger an Islamic uprising against the British in the

Middle East and even parts of India. However, by December such fears had receded. In Mesopotamia the British now poured in men and material ready for a major offensive that was launched on 13 December under the command of Maj Gen Sir Stanley Maude. In preparation for active operations, units were concentrated at forward defended camps on the Tigris such as Shaikh Saad. Forward of here were the opposing front lines where trench warfare was in progress. As Christmas approached, drafts for some units were still arriving. These troops were rushed up country as quickly as transport allowed:

I was allotted quarters in a tent with an officer named Large of the Warwickshire Regiment, and an Australian named Lee of the 36th Sikhs. Both very jolly chaps and we made the best of things, and we used to dine at night together, off the concoctions our batmen hashed up for us. Christmas Day 1916 came along, and we played bridge most of the day, and had a special dinner in the evening, with whisky and beer to wash it down, whilst the Ghurka band played carols. Now and again a rifle shot rang out from a watchful sentry, who thought he could see something moving in the desert.

Whilst in this camp the night was made hideous by the cries of hyenas and jackals, who faded away each morning at dawn, and when first heard reminded one of the wailing of lost souls. I had heard cats each night in England, but never anything like the row kicked up by these animals. (*2/Lt Frederick Brown, 7th Gloucesters*)

Along the Euphrates other units were also settling down to Christmas. They had played a more passive role during the campaign, guarding against possible Turkish moves towards Qurna at the confluence of the Euphrates and Tigris, the capture of which would cut Maude's supply line and threaten the oil refineries to the south. At the town of Nasiriyah, which had been in British hands since 25 July 1915, troops of the 15th Division were engaged in a round of garrison guard duty and training, including inter-company competitions in trench digging, range finding, pack-mule loading, fire control and night marching. In between such activity, Pte Henry White (1/5th Queens) found time to rear chickens and ducks for Christmas dinner. On 25 December, the long-awaited meal was preceded by the receipt of gifts from a number of the battalion's officers, many providing excellent additions to the coming meal:

We five orderlies received from Maj Relsall 5 bottles beer, 1 tin of peas, beans, Salmon, Tongue, chocolate and cigarettes, 3 packets of butterscotch and a cake. Capt Newland an autographic pocket Kodak between us.

Capt Smith a large ready cooked ham, from Asst Surgeon Cooper and Fanamdus 6 bottles of beer, some whisky and cigars, S&T Issue, pudding 8oz and cake 8oz from Daily News and Telegraph, and 4oz rum and 1 pint of beer. Regiment for us from Queens 4lb of pudding and 2 fowls. Ward Boys some fruit and a pudding (native) and some roasted almonds. Hospital cooks a cake. Some Christmas but feel very lonely wish I was at home with Liddle. Mail expected in today. Went to early service 8 o'clock, service and hymns at Hospital 3pm.

Xmas Dinner – Duck, green peas, roast potatoes. Plum pudding and custard, dried apricots, roast peanuts and beer. (*Henry White*)

However, in a land where sickness and disease were rife, not everyone was in a position to enjoy the festivities:

Dear All

Am unfortunately writing to you from a bed of sickness – nothing much simply a bad attack of diarrhoea, but enough of course to prevent me from enjoying my Xmas dinner . . .

The dinner I am giving the people here is as follows.

Soup
Fish Mayonnaise
Duck and Vegetables
Plum Pudding
Pate de Foie Gras
Asparagus
Sweets and Preserves

Rather a good dinner but unfortunately nothing that I can eat . . . You mustn't think we feed on the above scale every day. It is a special effort.

I wonder whether another Christmas will see me out here. I sincerely hope not.

The railway from Basra has now passed Safarh. And we have been busy for the last week unloading stores . . . chiefly good cheer for Christmas. Among this there were twelve large barrels of beer . . .

I've had plenty of time to think yesterday and today lying here doing nothing and most of my thoughts have turned homewards to past Christmases. I've seen myself waking up early in the morning and getting out of bed to receive my presents and give in exchange when funds ran to it. I've seen myself singing 'Christmas Awake' in the old parish church and the old rector in his fine voice and happy phrases wishing his flock a Merry Xmas. I have seen myself coming home and eating largely of goose and savoury pudding followed by numerous chocolates. I have seen myself relapsing temporarily into a state of coma and finally emerging to have a piece of Christmas cake at tea and so perhaps to a Christmas party.

Well, either next year or the year after I hope the same sort of Xmas will happen to me again. The actors will be older but the spirits will be there and that's the main thing.

Well here's to that next merry meeting. May it come sooner than we hope.

Ps: I find I have written quite a long letter. You'll have to thank the diarrhoea.[8] (*Capt Herbert Winn, 2/5th Gurkhas*)

While Maude gathered his forces on the Tigris, further pressure was being applied to the Turks by a British advance across the Sinai Desert. By the end of 1916, Gen Sir Archibald Murray's force had established a strong defensive position 100 miles east of the Suez Canal, so ending the Turkish threat to this vital imperial artery. Once established in this position Murray began to assess whether it would be feasible in the New Year to advance into Palestine and inflict a decisive defeat on the Turks. A key settlement occupied in Sinai was El Arish on the coastal plain. This became the main advance camp for the Egyptian Expeditionary Force (EEF) where men and matériel began to concentrate for the coming offensive:

We should have got in for Xmas Eve, but a great salt lake intervened: these areas are very dangerous, we often got our horses in up to the girths in the neighbourhood of the lakes and in places there are awful quicksands where horses entirely disappeared in a few minutes.

I therefore called a halt for the night, but when I rode round later on to see that the guards were properly placed, I went down to the lake and very carefully crossed not only the dried up bog, but the lake itself at a narrow part. It was quite firm and so exactly like a frozen lake in England very lightly coated with snow that I do not think anyone could distinguish between the two with the eye.

I had reveille sounded at 4 (or 0400 as we now have to write it) and consulted the native N.C.O.s as to the feasibility of taking a short cut across the lake. They were unanimous in declaring that the whole convoy would be swallowed up. I told them that nevertheless that was the route I intended to take and not a protest was raised. Whether their compliance was due to an unbounded confidence in my lucky star or to sheer helplessness to combat my pigheadedness I cannot say, but they followed to a man.

We had reached an island in the middle of the frozen lake when Xmas dawn broke: all the stars had faded except one wonderful star in the East, which had been a thing of great use to me as well as beauty in the campaign and which all the natives call THE STAR. In places the ice cracked and water oozed up through, but for the most part all was as firm as an arctic sea.

A great awe seemed to have come over man and beast. I halted and looked down the line, it was quite uncanny for there was neither sound nor motion . . . We might have been there for ages, frozen or bewitched. When I stalked on the ghostly procession followed soundlessly, and then weirder that all in this place of infinite solitude, music came from some near but invisible source: 'Adeste Fideles' and 'Hark! The Herald Angels', and about the same time there was a pulsation as of many wings overhead – a host of aeroplanes had turned out to see who was crossing the lake.

'Camel and camel man', an entry in the fancy dress competition of the 162nd Brigade, 54th (East Anglian) Division, held on Christmas morning 1916, at Ashton Post, part of the Suez Canal defence system. *(Q 57771)*

Men of the 31st Field Ambulance (RAMC) during a trip to the beach at Ra-el-Tin, near Alexandria, Christmas Day 1916. Pte L.E. Poulton, from whose collection the photograph comes, is standing second from the right. *(8004-27)*

Not a snowdrift but the aftermath of a sandstorm! Local labourers clear sand from a road near Sidi Bishr, Egypt, to allow the passage of an ambulance from the 31st Field Ambulance (RAMC), 1 January 1916. *(8004-27)*

Cases of Christmas foods from home are opened in the camp of the 127th Brigade's signals section (42nd Division), Egypt, December 1916. *(Private collection)*

An officer's servant lays out food and delicacies received by officers of the 127th Brigade's signals section (42nd Division), Egypt, December 1916. *(Private collection)*

The sun broke gloriously and soon we were in camp where a warm Xmas welcome and breakfast awaited us.

The day spent almost entirely in the saddle in the bracing air gave me a great zest for the Xmas dinner at 7.30 at which nearly all the officers in the neighbourhood – about twenty – were present. Bagpipes escorted the flaming pudding and natives masquerading as Father Xmas, Bloody Bill, Harlequin and Columbine etc played weird instruments at dessert as they processed round the board.[9] (*Lt Joseph McPherson, Egyptian Camel Transport Corps*)

In the Balkans too, December 1916 found British forces having advanced into contact with the enemy. The Bulgarian threat to Salonika had passed by May 1916, so Allied forces under French Gen Sarrail began moving north from their defensive lines towards the Greek–Serbian frontier along which the Bulgarians were entrenched. In August, when Sarrail launched his first offensive, spearheaded by French and Serbian troops, the British Salonika Force (BSF) under Lt Gen George Milne was holding a 90-mile front that included the wide, flat Struma Valley, which during summer was one of Europe's malarial blackspots, and the tangle of hills and ravines beside Lake Doiran, a position that German and Bulgarian military engineers had turned into a veritable fortress.

Later offensive pushes by French, Russian and Serbian forces placed the latter back on home soil with the liberation of Monastir on 19 November, the last major action before worsening winter weather conditions intervened. It would be spring 1917 before the BSF engaged in any major fighting, for in the final weeks of 1916 they simply tried to adapt to the wet and freezing conditions in the Macedonian wilderness, often with little more than a bivouac tent for shelter:

The weather was bitterly cold at this time, it being only a few days before Christmas, and we found it almost impossible to get any sleep in

Sorting the mail at a Field Post Office, Salonika, winter 1916. *(Q 32717)*

our 2 men bivvies. As a result, most of us spent the first night or two doubling up and down in a desperate effort to get warm. As the bivvies were open at each end there was no protection from the Arctic blast, so we resolved to think up some scheme for a new sleeping arrangement.

The state of the weather was such that men began to indulge in the unusual practice of volunteering for guard duty. The reason for this was that, instead of trying in vain to get to sleep in cold bivvies, members of the guard kept a very big fire going all night, and spent the time cooking porridge. The porridge was borrowed from the Company cooks, somewhat in advance of obtaining their permission. On the whole it was a very pleasant way to spend a cold night, except that in keeping out the cold we sat as close to the fire as possible, with the result that the heat stirred the lice into a frenzy of activity. We were, however, so accustomed to the activities of these boarders that we didn't worry too much. (*Pte Christopher Hennessey, 2/15th Londons*)

Men of the 11th Cameronians, 77th Brigade, 26th Division, receiving their Christmas mail, Salonika, December 1916. *(Q 31641)*

Capt Davis, Officer Commanding No.706 Motor Transport Company (ASC) carves the Christmas turkey for his officers in their tented Mess, Christmas Day 1916. No.706 MT Company was one of a number of support units attached to the Serbian Army during the Salonika Campaign. These units were fortunate to have the chance to celebrate Christmas twice each year, once on 25 December and again on 7 January, the latter date being Christmas Day to the Orthodox Serbs. *(Q 32622)*

Where the British had taken over trenches from the French there was much to be done to improve them in terms of defence and habitability. Undertaking this work during a Macedonian winter was difficult, so Christmas parcels arriving from home helped bring some cheer to proceedings. Capt Mervyn Sibly (9th Gloucesters) wrote to his sisters on Christmas Eve, just before his battalion moved to the advance line:

My dear Mildred and Enid
Thank you very much my dears for your many presents and all the trouble you have taken to brighten up my Christmas time. What a

wonderful cake that is, it is quite perfect. There are two classes of cakes in the world – those that you make and other cakes. Morton and Irwin both had so-called Christmas cakes and, though they were good, they were not fit to be seen in the next trench to mine. I cut the cake first on Thursday; Morton had to go up the line on Friday, with a fatigue party working on dugouts, and I said to him 'though I of course hoped nothing would happen to him one never knew, and we should both feel happier if he had some of my cake in his inside'. We had our first batch of mince pies on Thursday, and the second last night; Witts made quite a success of the pastry, so they, too, were 'top-hole'.

Crosse and Blackwell's tinned plum pudding was as nice as any I have tasted. I found a little sprig of prickly stuff, something like holly, with two red berries on and stuck it in the top then of a little brandy from someone's emergency brandy flask was emptied round the plate and we put it all burning on the table.

We have had to keep our Christmas a little in advance as we are going into trenches this evening. I must not write further or I may get late in packing my things up.

With much love to you both my 'best girls'

From their loving brother

Mervyn

Once in the trenches there was little activity as the enemy was also trying to have a quiet winter. Instead there was simply a need to establish routines to get them through the discomforts of trench life:

We came up to the first line on Sunday night – Christmas Eve – and took over the trenches on the extreme left of our sector; these are the trenches which extend from the Tributary Ravine to the west; on the lower slopes of Horseshoe Hill and opposite the ruined village of Doldzeli. The trenches are quite good for this part of the world and they need to be for there is no dugout accommodation and the men live in the trenches all the time. The officers have little dugouts in the side of the ravine the dimensions of mine where I am now writing are 5ft x 4ft 6ins by 3ft high. It would be a terrible little hole if it was wet but

A goal just about to be scored in an inter-company football match between teams from No. 706 Motor Transport Company (ASC), Christmas Day 1916. *(Q 32618)*

The winning team from No.706 Motor Transport Company (ASC) return for their Christmas party having won an inter-company football tournament, Christmas Day 1916. *(Q 32616)*

now the weather is fine it is not so bad and I can lie comfortably from corner to corner.

Thank God there was a wind today; yesterday the stench in this ravine was horrible. It comes from shallow refuse pits and shallower graves in fact I am told the legs of one dead Frenchman stick up above the ground just up the top of the bank; we must certainly put some more earth on top of him at night when we can go there unobserved.

I mentioned in another letter the parcels and letters I received on Boxing Day. The men were delighted to receive a good mail of Christmas parcels in the trenches . . .

This is really a bit of a rest cure – not very much work to do and the rest of the time, or greater part of it, I spend in my dugout sleeping or reading or writing in a recumbent position. I am a great believer in getting a proper amount of sleep in trenches. Many people seem to mess about doing nothing in particular when off duty and get haggard and cross through want of sleep.[10] (*Capt Mervyn Sibly*)

Soon after coming into contact with 'Johnny Bulgar' many in the BSF found him a sporting opponent who was keen to abide by the unwritten rules of the 'live and let live system'. Christmas provided a good test of this as Bulgaria, being an Orthodox country, celebrated on 7 January, which meant they could have regarded 25 December as just another day of the war. But this was generally not the case:

To-day is the Bulgar Christmas, and I have heard only some half-dozen shells of ours go over, for which I am glad, for they left us pretty quiet on Christmas Day, and it is only fair to do ditto.[11] (*Lt John Hammond, Medical Officer, 10th Devons*)

For those serving on the lines of communication or troops passing through the large transit camp called Summerhill, there was much more in the way of food and entertainment on offer thanks to the close proximity of depots and the 'bright lights' of the city of Salonika. Lt Holroyd Birkett Barker (134th Siege Battery, RGA) had just returned from hospital on Malta, where he had been recovering from malaria, and spent Christmas at Summerhill while awaiting re-posting to his unit:

Christmas Day under very unusual surroundings compels one to reflect upon the destiny that has led us here. We have very little work to do and after breakfast our main concern is to work up an appetite that will do justice to the dinner to be provided in the mess, which has been spoken of in very impressive tones during the last few days. At last the moment arrives, and we find ourselves in the mess hut – a long tin shed with a sandy floor, blankets hung along the sides for tapestry, forms to sit on, and candles stuck in old jam tins for illumination. Other tins are filled with soil and holly stands precariously in its midst; here and there red, white and blue paper is twisted . . . and at the head of the table appeared in an unsteady hand the word 'Welcome'. This completes the decorative element. We then turn on to soup – unnamed but apparently made from cayenne pepper – goose and turkey of most excellent flavour, a Christmas pudding and mince pics that are but vaguely reminiscent of the real thing and lastly jellies quite innocent of flavours and eaten, through pressure on the cutlery equipment, from a knife, oranges, nuts – but no crackers for them – other fruit that defies description.

What the function lacks in one department however is made up for by the general hilarity prevailing. Nature too is doing her best for the sun has been shining all day and a general warmth in the afternoon made a short walk along the plain very attractive. A discordant note was struck during the day that jarred upon the tranquil harmony of the scene, for two enemy aeroplanes appeared overhead apparently with the intention of bombing the town, and were vigorously fired at by anti-aircraft guns from all sites. Doubtless both of the opposing parties have attended Divine Service this morning and have hailed the Prince of Peace, and have then proceeded to pray for success for their respective arms, and are now sternly endeavouring to inflict slaughter upon each other. Surely only a Christian conscience can fail to detect an inconsistency in such a programme.

In the evening some promiscuous singing brings to a close a day that will no doubt be, throughout my life, memorable among the lengthening line of Christmases to come.

Not all Christmas dinners proved so memorable:

On Xmas Eve all Supply Officers of the ASC met for dinner at the White Tower – about 80 in all with various colonels and generals as guests. It was a most solemn and funereal affair . . . I had practically nothing to eat; I paid 15 francs for the ticket and probably have to pay another 10 for the champagne the guests drank, so zut, I do not think I shall patronize it next year. The worst of it was, I was opposite some new officers I had never seen before, and as we were at table for three hours, 8–11, conversation languished. What made it all the worse was loud applause from the next room, where 4 enticing Parisian ladies were dancing quadrilles with much display of lingerie. No, no more Xmas dinners at 30 francs for me.[12] (*2/Lt Eric de Normann, ASC Main Supply Depot*)

Following dinners, many units put on concerts of varying size and standards, many of which would have served to lift the spirits of even Lt de Normann:

Already a programme had been prepared and sent to print (per duplicator). A goodly number of the men had promised to contribute various items to the concert on Christmas night. A few boards had been 'found', and with these a rough-and-ready stage had been constructed at one end of the building which we used as 'dining-hall'. Then, the crowning achievement of all was the hiring of a piano from a Greek. Yes, wonder of wonders, a piano was obtainable even in Macedonia. You will believe me that its 'tone' was not quite perfect when I tell you that it was brought over three miles of bad roads to our camp, on a springless vehicle supplied by the ASC. Nevertheless, properly manipulated it produced 'some' music . . .

The first item on the programmes was a marching tune, excellently rendered on the piano by a certain Sgt-Maj. Then followed four or five songs, the audience joining in the chorus in each case. We also heard some good recitations, in which direction I also 'did my bit'. We were also fortunate in having an expert conjurer in the Company, who proved the truth of that oft-repeated statement, 'The quickness of the hand deceives the eye'. Then Sapper T gave us a turn; he could imitate almost any noise from the clucking of a broody-hen to the screeching of a circular-saw, and he had us all roaring with laughter before he sat down . . . Some of the men contributed short humorous stories. Volunteers were invited to step on stage and give a turn, and there was a big response.

Of course we couldn't close the meeting without the usual votes of thanks, after which we sang the National Anthem with great vigour. Then came a messenger and warned us there was likely to be an air-raid, so we popped off to bed, extinguishing all lights, and were soon in the land of dreams. Thus ended the happiest day I have yet spent on Active Service. Xmas Day, 1916, will always live in my mind as a 'Red letter day'.

NB – The 'air-raid warning' was a pre-arranged plan to get us all to bed quietly before eleven o'clock.[13] (*Sapper Albert Barker, Royal Engineers*)

While the opposing forces in the Balkans were beginning to test each other during 1916, final victory against German forces in Cameroon came in February, when Colonel Zimmermann's forces, numbering some 1,000 Germans, 6,000 Askaris and 7,000 civilians, crossed into Spanish Guinea. The survivors remained a force in being as the Spanish authorities were too weak to intern them. Zimmermann's plan was to await German victory in the war after which his troops would re-cross the border and re-establish German rule in Cameroon. Victory in West Africa left the Kaiser with just one colonial possession, German East Africa. Here, Gen Jan Smuts was given command in the spring of 1916. His first offensive saw the taking of Tanga (7 July) and Dar-es-Salaam (3 September), but attempts to surround and destroy von Lettow-Vorbeck's Schütztruppen proved a failure owing to the greater mobility of the German force, its knowledge of the terrain and acclimatisation; by May 1916, half the South African troops were down with disease. Smuts regrouped his forces ready for a second offensive in 1917. The high sick rates led to a decision to 'Africanise' the campaign, by bringing the Gold Coast and Nigeria

A column of troops and African bearers approaches a water camp on the Mikesse-Ruwu Road, German East Africa, December 1916. *(Q 15412)*

Regiments to East Africa. For a number the journey would cancel out any chance they had for a rest that Christmas:

I have not had much time to write lately as I have been moving very rapidly since Xmas Eve when I left Dar-es-Salaam. We had a nine hour journey by rail starting early in the afternoon so arriving about midnight. I luckily travelled in a wooden van with eleven other fellows but there were three iron vans with about the same number of whitemen in each. The heat during the day in these things is awful.

We started trekking on Xmas afternoon and did about 16 miles and dossed down on the roadside about 11am. It was quite enough for most people as we were all pretty soft after a long voyage. I had lent my valise to a fellow whose bedding was lost on the road as I had a camp bed and blankets and about 2am a heavy tropical rain storm came on and my bed was very soon 6 inches deep in water. I was too tired to turn out and slept off and on till dawn. We had only a short march next day and then a day off to dry our kit. Mine only consists of a change of clothes, bedding and a few cooking pots. The following day we did 16 miles and slept 45 whitemen packed like sardines in one shelter as it was raining again . . .

So far the rations are quite good but of course when one is in action their arrival is very uncertain but so far we have had at least one meal a day. The supply of drinking water is very difficult as it is very risky to drink any water one comes across and we are tied down to an absolute minimum of carriers.[14] (*Capt Eric Barclay, 4th Nigeria Regiment*)

For those on the lines of communication in East Africa matters could be rather more comfortable. Sapper Frank Rowland (Royal Engineers, Signals Section) was based for over a year at Dodoma railway station. Here the signallers worked in the German-built railway offices and occupied native-built huts. A stationary hospital was also on site. Rations remained somewhat limited, Rowland saving a tin of sardines as a treat with which to celebrate his birthday on 19 December. Even so:

A troop train en route from Dar-es-Salaam to Mikesse, December 1916. It was on one such train that Capt Eric Barclay moved up-country during Christmas 1916. He was lucky to travel in a wooden truck rather than the metal ones depicted. Owing to the heat inside these wagons, six men from each were allowed to ride on the roofs during daylight hours. *(Q 15414)*

It was a pleasant change to mix with a larger number of troops, to frequent and buy from the expeditionary force canteens and the Greek and Arab shops in the native quarter. There was a church marquee and a padre. Mail came frequently . . . Christmas 1916 was celebrated happily, and there was even a rum ration on New Year's Day 1917. I visited comrades in hospital and lived a life of a soldier in a barrack town in England. But there was still plenty to remind us where we were – native troop movements on the railway, native women with the troops, carrying babies and military stores as they left the trains and marched southward.

Commercially produced, sentimental Christmas card produced in 1916, showing a soldier carrying mistletoe and his wife beside a heavily laden Christmas tree. (*Private collection*).

·M·Q·
47· INFANTRY·
BDE·
·MENU·

Oysters
Soup
Fish
Roast Turkey
Roast Potatoes
  Cauliflower

  ·Plum Pudding

 Devilled Liver

Cheese

Dessert

Coffee

XMAS·1917·

Menu card produced for the dinner enjoyed by officers of 47 Infantry Brigade Headquarters on Christmas Day 1917 in rest billets at Tincourt near Peronne on the Somme. (*Private collection*).

Christmas card produced by the Royal Naval Division in 1916, making light of trench conditions on the Somme that winter and showing the advantage of having a naval background! The card was printed in Paris by Gr. Devambez, 63 Passage des Panoramas. (*MISC 209 /3047*)

Royal Naval Division

France 1916

Up Anchor!
(Ancre)

Artwork from inside a Christmas card produced by the XV Army Corps in 1916, showing the activity of both front line and support troops of the Corps. (*Lt Col O M Lanyon collection 92/19/1*).

Christmas card produced by the 46th (North Midland) Division in 1917, showing a group of soldiers illuminated by a 'Very light' as they cross No Man's Land. The card was published by George Falkner & Sons, 170 Deansgate, Manchester. (*2/Lt E H Bennett collection 79/35/1*).

Christmas card produced by the Royal Engineers CME (Light Railway) Workshops in France, 1918, showing Kaiser Wilhelm II being knocked over by a British light railway locomotive. (*Canon R L Hussey collection P 452*).

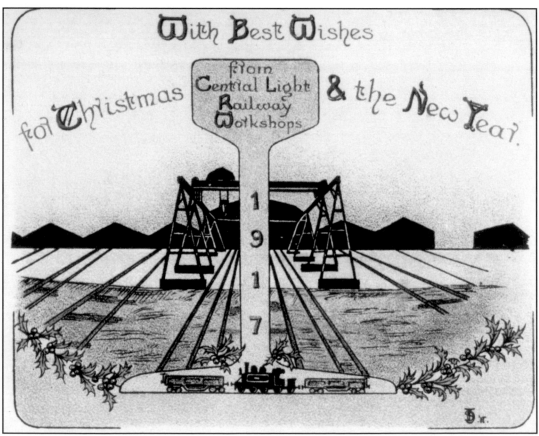

Christmas card produced by the Central Light Railway Workshops (Royal Engineers) in France, 1917. (*Canon R L Hussey collection P 452*)

Christmas card celebrating Christmas 1918 and the end of the campaign in Macedonia. The motif shows a member of the British Salonika Force holding a Turk in his right hand and a Bulgarian soldier in his left. 'Johnny' was a standard term of reference used by people in the Balkans and near east to refer in conversation to strangers from English speaking countries. It was quickly adopted by British soldiers with 'Johnny Turk' and 'Johnny Bulgar' becoming standard slang for their opponents in Macedonia, Gallipoli and the Middle East. The card was produced by the 8th Field Survey Company, Royal Engineers. (*Private collection*)

Artwork from the inside of a Christmas card produced by the Royal Naval Division in 1917. The card was published by Gr Devambez, 63 Passage des Panoramas, Paris. (*MISC 209/3047*).

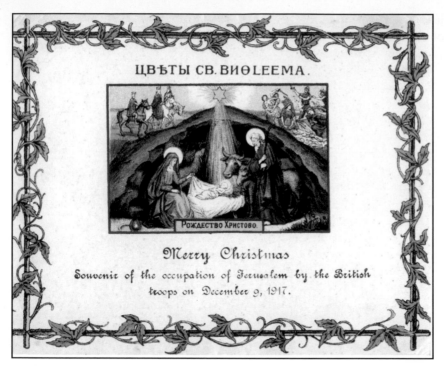

Christmas card produced as a souvenir of the occupation of Jerusalem by British forces on 9 December 1917. (*MISC 74/1113*).

Humorous artwork from the Christmas card produced for the 11th Division, showing a surprised British soldier raiding the enemy lines just as a rather portly German arrives carrying numerous bottles of 'Christmas Cheer'! (*Lt Col O M Lanyon collection 92/19/1*)

Christmas card produced by BEF General Headquarters, France, 1918. (*Capt P M Sharp collection 78/69/1*).

Christmas card produced by the 53rd Battalion, Australian Imperial Force, in 1918. This unit was formed in Egypt on 14 February 1916 as part of the expansion of the AIF. Half of the men were veterans of Gallipoli, having served in the 1st Battalion, the rest were new volunteers from Australia. Reflecting the composition of the 1st Battalion, the 53rd was mostly composed of men from the suburbs of Sydney. They arrived in France on 27 June 1916 and fought at Fromelles on 19 July, suffering 625 casualties. The battalion gained the nickname 'the Whale Oil Guards' during the winter of 1916–17 after their CO Lt Col Oswald Croshaw ordered troops to polish their helmets for a parade with whale oil, which had been issued as a preventative against trench foot. (*Private collection*)

A 1917 Christmas card produced by 54th (East Anglian) Division bearing the formation's campaign honours of Gallipoli, Egypt and Palestine. (*Private collection*).

Christmas card produced for the 56th (London) Division in 1917. The four battle honours wrapped round the holly record the Division's major actions on the Western Front during 1916 and 1917. (*Private collection*)

Certificate given to school children across the British Empire by the Overseas Club as a reward for sending a Christmas parcel to a serving soldier or sailor, 1916. (*MISC 192/2846*).

Christmas 1917

I send to all ranks of the Navy and Army my hearty good wishes for Christmas and New Year. I realize your hardships patiently and cheerfully borne and rejoice in the success you have won so nobly. The Nation stands faithfully to its pledges, resolute to fulfil them. May God bless your efforts and give us victory. Our Christmas thoughts are with the sick and wounded sailors and soldiers. We know by personal experience with what patience and cheerfulness their suffering is borne. We wish all a speedy restoration to health, a restful Christmastide and brighter days to come.

The King's Christmas Message to his Troops, 1917

As 1917 drew to an end the Allies were in a position of strength despite the collapse into revolution of Russia during November. The Germans' launching of unrestricted submarine warfare and withdrawing to the Hindenburg Line position (March–April 1917) were admissions that the fighting on the Somme and at Verdun in 1916 could not be sustained for another year. The U-boat campaign drew the USA into the war against Germany and with it gave a huge advantage in terms of raw materials, manufacturing power and manpower to the Allies. To make matters worse for Germany, by late 1917 the U-boat campaign had failed, defeated by the Royal Navy's anti-submarine measures, including the introduction of a convoy system for merchant shipping. On the Western Front pressure had been maintained on the Germans. On 9 April the British opened the Battle of Arras, in support of the French 'Nivelle Offensive'. The Canadian Corps took Vimy Ridge and during the initial fighting the British 3rd Army also made inroads into the Hindenburg Line. However, stalemate returned as fighting dragged on until mid-May,

A light covering of snow covers the position of a 6-in Howitzer on the Cambrai sector of the front, 21 December 1917. Following the 1914 and limited 1915 Christmas truces, commanders on both sides were always determined to keep the artillery firing to prevent such unwarlike behaviour from occurring again. *'We had a fall of snow on Xmas day but it didn't stop the strafe a bit and they were going hammer and tongs for hours.'* (ACM *Frank Haylett, No. 42 Kite Balloon Section, RFC) (Q 10594)*

and Gen Nivelle's much-vaunted offensive on the Chemin des Dames, which opened on 16 April, was a total failure. This defeat broke the morale of the French Army and led to widespread mutinies that lasted until the autumn. From this time Haig's BEF became the main offensive force on the Western Front.

In the summer of 1917, Haig launched an offensive in Flanders. Heralded by the explosion of nineteen large mines under German positions on Messines Ridge, the offensive known as the Third Battle of Ypres, or more popularly Passchendaele, got under way on 31 July. However, with over 4 million shells having been fired in the preparatory artillery bombardments, the ground over which the infantry was expected to advance was badly torn up. After four weeks many of the initial objectives were not taken and torrential rains set in, turning the battlefield into a quagmire. A change in tactics, bringing in 'Bite and Hold' operations to win limited objectives met with some success. But with increasingly poor weather conditions, the battle degenerated into a slogging match with both sides losing something in the region of 250,000 men by the time Haig halted operations following the capture of Passchendaele Ridge in November.

If the Germans believed this to be the end of major operations for 1917, they reckoned without Haig's willingness to employ novel tactics in a final attempt to pierce the Hindenburg Line before the New Year. On 20 November, over hard, chalky, open fields near Cambrai, 300 tanks led 6 British divisions forward. Surprise was achieved and early gains were made. But the loss of 179 tanks on the first day, with few reserves available, slowed the advance as German resistance stiffened. Nine days after the attack began, Haig called a halt to the battle. The British had created a vulnerable salient, which they were preparing to evacuate when

Officers of the RGA observing the German lines from the cover of frost-covered shrubs, Cambrai sector, 21 December 1917. *'Winter has set in with a vengeance, everything is frozen absolutely solid and I don't think I have ever seen such a glorious picture as all the trees in the orchards about here now present. It is one magnificent fairyland, all the branches are covered in frost-spikes nearly an inch long. It is simply beautiful!' (ACM Frank Haylett, No. 42 Kite Balloon Section, RFC)* (Q 10596)

Officers engaged in a snowball fight near Hesdin on the Western Front, 19 December 1917. *'On Christmas Eve 1917, with our company commander on leave, the Sergeant Major suggested we led a snowball attack on the officers. However, the officers had precisely the same idea, ambushing us as we approached the farmhouse where a real fight ensued in which an officer was knocked backwards into a filthy midden by a snowball I planted between his eyes. This terminated the battle and the officers invited us in for a welcome drink.'* (QMS Frederick Hunt, 203rd Machine Gun Company, MGC) (Q 8343)

German troops counter-attacked. When fighting ended on 7 December, the front line was back in a similar position to where it had been before the British attack.

Active operations were over for another year and the troops prepared themselves to face yet another winter in the trenches:

The damp and verminous trenches harboured disease; but all possible precautions against it were taken. Not only were there gum-boots, grease and regular changes of socks; but Maj-Gen Gorringe, the divisional commander, most wisely insisted that the men in the trenches should have a hot meal or a hot drink every four hours. Huge food containers, manufactured on the principle of the Thermos bottle, were used for that purpose and the battalion cookers were brought right up to Ravine Wood, within six hundred yards of the German front line. (*Capt Sir George Clarke, 1/8th Londons*)

In the Ypres Salient, so much fought over since the summer of 1917, men in the line met Christmas as best they could:

We spent our Christmas day up there in the shell holes and pill boxes. A Happy Xmas, yes, but we didn't see Father Xmas come down the chimney with a big bag of toys, or any presents on his back . . . we went into the line on 22nd Dec. and we came out of it again on the 29th Dec. at 9 o'clock at night. We had a white Xmas here and it

Artwork from the inside of a Christmas card produced by the Royal Naval Division in 1917. The card was published by Gr Devambez, Passage des Panoramas 63, Paris. (*MISC 209/3047*)

Men of the 15th Royal Scots having dinner in a trench near Croisselles, 4 January 1918. *(Q 10607)*

began to snow on Xmas eve, and we had about six weeks of it. It kept on freezing day and night all the time, and we were snowed up and frozen up then, but we had our happy Xmas day on New Year's Day after coming out.

Our Christmas dinner in the line or shell holes was composed of tins of bully beef and a few hard biscuits thrown into a canteen, with a big handful of snow to make water. We could make some Bully Stew for dinner that day and we enjoyed it fine, as there was nothing else to have at that time. Snow the only thing we could use to make water as we couldn't use the water in our bottles we carried for it. It was a crime then which would have won us 14 days pay stopped, and we didn't want that now.

The ground was covered in snow and the water in the shell holes was frozen. We were not supposed to use it or drink it at any time. We had to be very careful about lighting a fire because of the smoke in the daytime and the light of the fire at night as well. If Jerry had seen it we may have had a gentle visitor come over to visit and wish us a Happy Xmas and a Xmas box to wish us a Happy New Year all in one day then. So we had to make ourselves happy but not seen too much at any time. (*Pte Alfred Lewis, 6th Northamptons*)

Some units were doubly unlucky in spending both Christmas and New Year in the line. One of these was the 14th Argyll & Sutherland Highlanders who were back at Clonnel Camp, Hamelincourt, when they received Christmas parcels from the people of Stirling on 19 December and enjoyed a seasonal dinner four days later. On Christmas Eve they relieved the 13th Yorkshires of 121st Brigade in the line at Fontaine-les-Croisilles, where they remained until the evening of 27 December, when the 16th Royal Scots took their place. Two days later the Argylls found themselves back in trenches, this time the Bullecourt section support line, where they remained into the New Year:

A working party from the 13th Royal Welch Fusiliers filling sandbags during the construction of dugouts in trenches near Fleurbaix, 28 December 1917. (*Q 8372*)

We really had a good time just before Christmas and I put away one cake and other good things . . . but . . . as I sit and shiver tonight I think of the stuff we wasted there. After expecting to spend Christmas 'out' we were quite disappointed when we got the order to pack up before the eventful day and let me but whisper it we spent New Year 'in' too. Rotten luck we thought to have both days 'in' but thank goodness we were in a quiet spot and everybody returned safely except for a few who are now secretly gloating in Blighty at our sad fate. I am sorry in a way I am not in that select body myself but I am bad enough already without Old Fritz modelling my torso. As I have said before let me return as I am.

The weather is now of the vilest, after having had hard frost since my return a thaw set in and today water and all its discomforts are with us.[1] (*Pte Robert Lawson, 14th Argyll & Sutherland Highlanders*)

Australian troops enjoy warming mugs of cocoa at an Australian Comforts Fund Canteen housed in a shell-damaged building near Ploegsteert in the Ypres Salient, 26 December 1917. *(E(AUS) 1458)*

As in previous years there were those who were more fortunate:

Many thanks for your nice letter and kind wishes. May I return
the compliment and wish you and Cicely the nicest Christmas and
happiest New Year possible. We look like having a really nice Xmas
for once in a way out here. We are out of the trenches in a little village
just behind the lines and we shall be here for Xmas day too. Anyway
we are making terrific preparations, making tables and forms for the
men's dinner, killing pigs and roasting and buying beer and vegetables
for them. There will be such a feed and drink as never was and a
concert after. I only hope they will not be too drunk to sing. As for the
officers we have a Turkey and about 14 Xmas puddings to say nothing

A British field artillery battery passes through the snow-covered ruins of Ypres,
22 December 1917. *(Q 9806)*

Officers of the Royal Field Artillery with their Christmas mail bag, December 1917. (Q 8346)

of 6 orange puddings and soup tins and tinned Turkey, 12 cakes, 14 tins of shortbread, chocolate and sweets galore. In fact we have a miniature grocer's shop. I expect we shall be horribly ill after it all and be awfully snappy the next day but still we must do something.[2] (*2/Lt Harold Ridsdale, 76th Field Company, RE*)

The sappers held their company Christmas celebrations on 24 December and the event was evidently a success, their war diary recording that they spent the following day 'recovering from Christmas dinner'.[3] On Boxing Day the company marched to Stirling Camp near Hervin Farm in preparation for work on a new set of trenches. But not every soldier had fond memories of their unit's communal festivities:

Well Old Dear how did you spend your Christmas, I hope it was a better one than I did for I think it was the worse one I have ever spent.

I was thinking of you all and wishing that I was with you all, and I was very much with you at 8.00, oh yes, I drank your health at that time. After that time I went for a good walk to get out of it. Why, well some of them had got too much beer down them and they were playing H——. Yes it was a fine idea clubbing together to have a feed, it might have been if the money had been spent right. We got together 105 francs and the army canteen fund gave us 50 so we put 80 to it for two turkeys that was going to be got for us in Paris and the rest of the money was spent on a barrel of beer which was alright for those who drank it, our officer bought us 5 bottles of wine, which was very good of him. That was all the chaps who did not drink had

A Royal Engineers motorcyclist in deep snow on the Hesdin–St Pol road, 19 December 1917. This is one of a series of official photographs showing members of the BEF with a Christmas pudding. They were obviously taken for propaganda value to raise morale at home by showing that the British Tommy was cheerfully celebrating the festive season despite the hardships of war. *(Q 8339)*

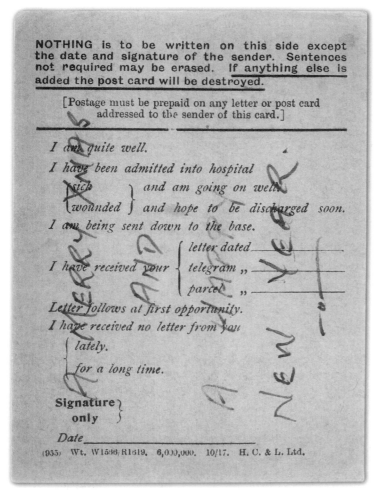

NOTHING is to be written on this side except the date and signature of the sender. Sentences not required may be erased. If anything else is added the post card will be destroyed.

[Postage must be prepaid on any letter or post card addressed to the sender of this card.]

I am quite well.

I have been admitted into hospital

{ sick } and am going on well

{ wounded } and hope to be discharged soon.

I am being sent down to the base.

I have received your { letter dated_____

{ telegram „ _____

{ parcel „ _____

Letter follows at first opportunity.

I have received no letter from you

{ lately.

{ for a long time.

Signature }
only }

Date_____

(935) Wt. W1586/R1619. 6,000,000. 10/17. H. C. & L. Ltd.

A British field postcard sent to Miss C. Latimer, 4 Rowley Road, Harringay, London, on 24 December 1917, bearing the hand-written message 'A Merry Xmas and a Happy New Year'. Christmas was the only time when a personal message could be written on such cards. At all other time the sender had simply to delete the set sentences not applicable to his situation, sign and date the card, otherwise it would be destroyed. *(MISC 91/1330)*

for their money. Well the turkeys did not turn up but the money did at ¼ 9 on Christmas Eve. So we had a bit of beef for dinner which I think was just as good. We also had ½ a pound of pudding which was very nice. The dinner was the last part of the day, for when the beer got going the trouble got going as well, so I cleared out just after 8 . . . at that time things were not so bad, but two of them play hot stuff until ½ 2 in the morning so to end it we got out of bed and put them to sleep. I never want to spend another day like it . . . Well the money that was sent back to us we are having a feed on New Years Day (but no beer). We gave 50 francs to a chap to spend and I must say he has spent it well. We have got two chickens for dinner on that day and he has bought a lot of things that otherwise we do not get and we have still 30 francs in hand, which we are thinking of buying some records for the gramophone with. So I think we shall have a better time on New Years than we did on Christmas Day.[4] (*Sapper Jim Sams, 1st Army, 3rd Area Detachment, Signals Company, RE*)

In the camps dotted about villages and woods behind the lines, much effort went into organising sporting events of various kinds. Football was particularly popular whether it be against another battalion, at inter-company level, or officers versus sergeants. Of the latter matches, unit war diaries record that the sergeants invariably came out victorious. Boxing, rugby, athletics and horse shows were also popular. Other, more ad hoc, events provided more comedic than sporting entertainment, both for the audience and those taking part:

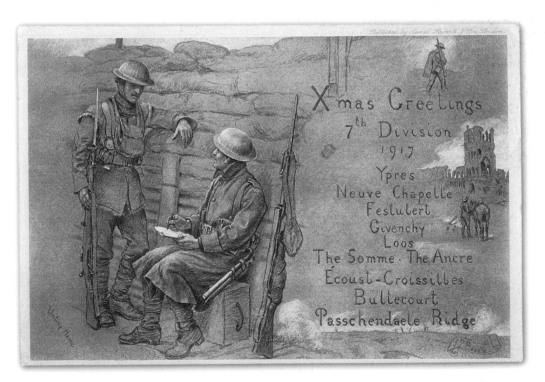

Christmas card produced by the 7th Division in 1917, showing a soldier writing home from the trenches. The card was published by James Haworth & Brothers, London. (*J.B. Milne collection 87/51/1*)

Christmas card produced by the 30th Division in 1917, showing a sentry using a trench periscope to look over a wintry No Man's Land. This is another of the detailed artwork cards published by James Haworth & Brothers, London. *(Lt Col O.M. Lanyon collection 92/19/1)*

Christmas card produced by the 46th (North Midland) Division in 1917, showing a group of soldiers illuminated by a Very light as they cross No Man's Land. The card was published by George Falkner & Sons, 170 Deansgate, Manchester. *(2/Lt E.H. Bennett collection 79/35/1)*

After lunch came the gymkhana. About 15 of us went down to theatre and dressed up. I was M.F.H. with a long black coat, white flannels, gum boots, old top hat, spurs, eyeglass and riding whip . . .

At 2.30 we mounted horses in market square and proceeded to move off. One horse started to gallop stable wards, so did mine. Then the fun began, all the horses with dressed people galloping along road some controlled others not, mine was being given its head, found its stable. I decided to return to scene of action, did so, found it necessary to return to stable and once more back to riding ring. We then had tug-of-war on horseback. I did not intend entering but owing to backwardness of others I did so, still in costume. I was finally persuaded to enter for wrestling on bare horseback. I had a new mount which had a very prominent backbone. My first opponent was a heavy little fat man, we struggled and to my unbounded surprise, I found he was pulled off.

Elated with victory I was about to seek fresh victims when suddenly my mount began rearing about, and I took a delightful toss over his head and my part in the show was finished.[5] (*2/Lt Winn Johnstone-Wilson, 10th Royal Sussex*)

In large towns and cities further back behind the lines, such as Amiens and Arras, there were correspondingly more varied entertainments to hand:

The entertainments of the place were many, the leading one being a pantomime (*The Babes in the Wood*), being run at the original Theatre of Arras, which was drawing larger crowds than any theatre could draw here. Then there was a certain Divisional Troupe . . . in some old French cavalry barracks who gave an extremely good show and changed their programme every week. Good parties were also to be seen at The St George's Hall, which was also a YMCA. Also at either one or two

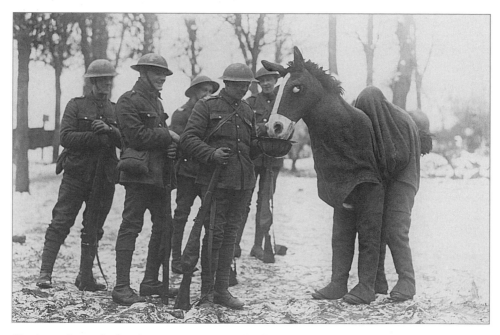

During rehearsals for the pantomime *Cinderella*, the 'horse' takes time out to meet his public, 2 January 1918. This particular version of *Cinderella* was put on by a concert part from a RFC Kite Balloon Section based near Bapaume on the Somme. (*Q 8382*)

Christmas card produced by the 24th Division in 1917, showing the Imperial German eagle being plucked by Allied soldiers. *(Private collection)*

places you could see a good show of pictures . . . (*Pte Fred Philipson, 1st Grenadier Guards*)

But no matter where and when soldiers had a chance to celebrate Christmas out of the line, they took full advantage of the break from army routine and the more relaxed attitude taken to discipline. In 1917 this was particularly true for those who had fought through the recently concluded Third Battle of Ypres and the Battle of Cambrai:

Tuesday 25 December:

It began to feel a bit more like Xmas last night, when I was in bed waiting for the goddess of sleep to visit me, I heard a band in the distance playing Xmas carols. It was lovely in the morning to be in bed and feel that there was no necessity to get up at all if you don't want to and I didn't until nearly 9am. Then I dressed in all my gladrags, no working clothes on a real holiday and strolled into breakfast.

We had tinned kidneys and tinned mushrooms for breakfast and very good they were. After breakfast I sat in the Mess and read my Xmas mail . . . The Mess dinner was a great success the cooks really did wonderful work. We visited all the huts and drank all their healths and by the time we had finished we had imbibed not too wisely but too well. Our own dinner was in the evening. We had invited the supply officer to dine with us and French of the CDM company came too so we were a merry party. The turkey was excellent so was Walford's plum pudding. After dinner the sergeants came over and serenaded us so we had them all into the Mess and had quite a rowdy evening. It was lucky I think that Xmas only comes once a year. It snowed during the afternoon and evening – real proper Xmas weather. The war didn't quite stop, our guns were firing slowly all afternoon and we had some observation balloons up but things were comparatively quiet. (*Capt Eustace Vachell, Royal Engineers*)

Christmas 1917 on the Western Front was also marked by a relatively unknown, violent incident behind British lines when men of No. 151 Company, Chinese Labour Corps, killed their British sergeant major, who had been extorting money and flogging labourers under his charge. Most of the Chinese were easily rounded up by British troops near Reninghelst, though others fled towards 5 Corps HQ at Locre:

Went to HQ for Xmas dinner and tea. After dinner we went over to the football ground to see a match at 3pm, but the Chinese coolies encamped just opposite put a stop to it. They murdered their NCOs and fled the camp armed with sticks, iron and tops of picks. They came across our ground and then the artillery camp turned out and

This concert was a joint production by the 1st and 15th Auxiliary Omnibus Companies. (*J.B. Milne collection 87/51/1*)

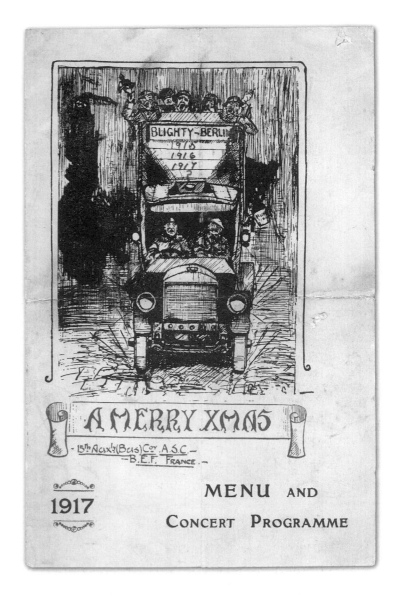

commenced firing rifles at them. Several shots missed me by not much! The Police sent us all back to camp to get our rifles and we all had to turn out and shoot Chinese to help stop the mutiny. About 8 were shot on our footer ground. Some had got very far away and we had to help round them up. In all we captured 93 prisoners! *Some* Xmas believe me! In evening, I went back by the longest way instead of the short cut which is past the Chinese camp and through the woods. Got caught in heavy snowstorm. (*Signaller David Doe, 51st Signal Company, RE*)

This was the culmination of unrest among Chinese labourers, which had begun in September 1917 with a contractual dispute in which labourers demanded danger money when they believed they would have to work within German artillery range. At Dunkirk, large numbers of labourers fled their camp after an air raid and refused to return to work for four days. In October further disturbances occurred over harsh levels of discipline being used against the Chinese. To quell the affair five labourers were shot dead and fourteen wounded. Matters remained serious, with a similar incident taking place at Fontinettes between 16 and 23 December. Once again armed guards opened fire during attempts to quell the disturbance. News of the troubles got into the British press, where they came to the attention of Chinese government representatives in London. Work was put in hand by the Director of Labour, Brig Gen Evan Gibb, under strong representations from Lt Col Fairfax, organiser of the Chinese Labour Corps. These addressed the staffing of labour units with officers and NCOs who understood the Chinese and looked to remove disaffection felt over living conditions, poor facilities and pay. Such serious incidents did not occur again.

December 1917 also found troops of six British divisions (5th, 7th, 21st, 23rd, 41st and 48th) deployed in Italy. They had been sent, along with six French divisions, from the Western Front to help shore up the Italian Army, which had been severely shaken by the Austro-German attack at Caporetto (24 October 1917). In the following month, Italian forces were pushed back 80 miles to the River Piave, during which time the Italian 2nd Army ceased to exist as a fighting force. By the time the front stabilised in mid-November, the first British and French troops were arriving on Italian soil. First into the line were the British 23rd and 41st Divisions who relieved Italian troops along the Piave between 30 November and 4 December. They were to find northern Italy a pleasant change from France and Flanders. Views of dramatic snow-capped mountains, wooded slopes and wide rivers combined with a lower-intensity war. This was especially true after the Austro-German offensive ceased in early December and German units were withdrawn for service on the Western Front. During December the 23rd Division suffered only 121 casualties and the 41st Division a correspondingly low figure of 158.

For the rest of the British force, Christmas 1917 was spent in reserve, allowing time to acclimatise to their new surroundings:

I had a very strenuous day the other day. I took my staff which consists of 4 officers and 6 sergeants and others. We rode about 30 miles on horses, climbed one hill of 1000 feet and another of 4000 feet to the heavy snows – it was intensely cold – only 4 of us got to the top. As it was late we came down in an empty Italian lorry along one of those great spiral military roads recently made – it took 1 hour 10 mins to do 22 miles downhill. It was only about 2 miles straight up. I really don't know how the Italian soldiers stand the awful cold. One Italian soldier gave me the Edelweiss which I enclose for you – with my love (from Italy at Christmas).

Now we are training hard and we need it – warfare is so different out here to what it was in France. I like this life for a change. The Colonel

A machine gunner, who has been busy plucking turkeys ready for Christmas, carries two more birds destined for the pot, Italy, December 1917. *(Q 26539)*

has been very nice and leaves me alone to carry on how I like. The horses are looking well in spite of the cold weather and the snow.[6] (*Capt Archibald Laporte-Payne, 175 Brigade, RFA*)

With the majority of units behind the front line, most British troops were able to spend a relatively relaxed Christmas and, being Italy, wine flowed freely:

We spent our Xmas 1917 amongst French and Italian troops, so we got merry with plenty of wine. I was a bit in the forefront, being able to speak French and we finished up with mixed dancing among the troops. We were twice a week on guard . . . It was indeed long nights with intense cold and snow and freezing hard. It was fine during the day with the hot sun and white carpet, for the atmosphere is dry. Many reported sick with their blood out of order, and the medical officer remarked it was by drinking too much fresh wine. (*Gnr Edmund Lenfestey, 35th Battery, 22nd Brigade, RFA*)

In places the chance was also taken to play a little international football. The 8th Royal Warwicks beat a regiment of French Chasseurs 8–0, though in the return match the French, who had been practising hard, only lost 3–2.[7] Although at a respectable distance behind the front line, the British were, on occasion, reminded that they had not come to Italy on a rest cure:

Christmas Day: Breakfast – bacon, rissoles and porridge. Dinner – pork roast, beef roast and potatoes. We were to have had turnips but they were all bad. Christmas pudding with rum sauce and a pint of vino for each man but it was horrible, rough and sour so hardly anyone drank it. Sgts drunk again so I had the biggest part of their dinners and all their pudding. Harris and I went for a walk along the Brenta in the morning, intending to go to a small town we could see about three miles away. After we had gone a couple of miles we heard a familiar whining noise and then a crash and although we had heard thousands of shells before, it quite startled us as it was the last thing we expected

An Italian girl helps men of a company from the MGC pluck turkeys and geese for their Christmas dinner, December 1917. *(Q 26537)*

on a quiet Christmas morning for we had been told we were at least 8 to 10 miles from the line, so we asked an Italian what it was and it turned out to be an Austrian long range gun shelling this town of Bassano. We often watched it after but that morning we didn't want our appetites upset so we turned off and had a lift to Marostica, another town near us and so home. *(Pte Albert Bullock, 8th Royal Warwicks)*

The British also quickly developed a warm rapport with the Italian civilian population. For example, the war diary of the 1/4th Royal Berkshires records of their stay at San Croce-Bigolina in December 1917:

During the month the welcome from the ITALIANS has grown more cordial and we are receiving great kindness from them. As soon as they got to know us, they will do anything to help us that we ask and quite a good feeling now exists between us; the Parish Priest especially doing everything he can to help us.

On Christmas Day the priest assisted by giving over the largest room in his house as Battalion HQ Mess, where all the officers dined together in the evening, using all the crockery that he could provide for them. The men of the battalion dined earlier in the day, with 'A', 'C' and 'D' Companies eating by companies and 'B' Company by platoons, while HQ staff, the battalion band, stores and transport staff ate separately. Extras, such as pork, fruit, beer, coffee and vegetables were provided by the officers through subscriptions in proportion to their pay:

> In addition a very kind letter was received from the Secretary of the County Association enclosing a cheque for £50 raised by the President, Members of the Berkshire Territorial Force Association and some of the residents of Berkshire for the provision of Christmas gifts for the men. The Association wished the CO and all ranks the very best of good wishes for Christmas and the New Year and a telegram to this effect was also received. (*War Diary 1/4th Royal Berkshires*)

Gifts were also organised for British troops by the Italian Touring Club, the distribution of those for the 5th and 48th Divisions (XI Corps) took place at Piazzolo on 23 December. One officer and nine men represented each infantry battalion; there were also representatives from other units such as artillery and transport. The selected troops were formed up in four lines on three sides of the town square. At 2.20 p.m. a car carrying Lt Gen Sir Richard Haking (XI Corps commander) and senior members of the Touring Club pulled into the square. The 5th Division band struck up the Italian national anthem and all troops presented arms. This was followed by the British national anthem after which Haking thanked the Italian Touring Club for their kindness in arranging for the presentation of gifts, which consisted of a dictionary, pocket book, chocolates and bar of soap for each man. After a marchpast, the troops gave three cheers for Italy and then returned to their respective parade grounds from where they were dismissed.

Across the Adriatic, men of the BSF were settling in for another Christmas in the Balkans, either in the wilds of the Macedonian countryside, where few comforts were on hand, or in the large base camp area around Salonika. The year had seen the first major action fought by Milne's troops, namely the First Battle of Doiran (24–25 April and 8–9 May 1917). This was in support of a Franco-Serbian offensive west of the River Vardar in which the Allied commander, Gen Sarrail, hoped to decisively break the Bulgarian line. For their part the men of XII Corps were to pin Bulgarian units to the maze of trenches in the hills around the town of Doiran, thus preventing them moving west of the Vardar. This aim was achieved at a price of 5,024 casualties, although ultimately it proved a wasted effort as Sarrail's offensive failed to achieve anything close to a breakthrough. Failure led to the removal, during the summer of 1917, of the 10th (Irish) and 60th (London) Divisions to Palestine, where Gen Sir Edmund Allenby was building up forces for a major offensive

Members of the 22nd Divisional concert party The Macedons at the village of Rates, behind the Doiran front, Christmas 1917. The Macedons were formed by 2nd Lts John 'Jess' Spyer and Derek Oldham. At this time, Spyer was serving as a subaltern with 'C' Company, 7th South Wales Borderers. He was formerly organist at the Royal Military Academy Chapel, Sandhurst, a post to which he returned after the First World War. *(PC 1202)*

against the Turks. One point in favour of the Allies in the Balkans was the entry of Greece into the war on 29 June, following the abdication of King Constantine. The availability of Greek troops went some way to offsetting the Allied manpower shortage in the Balkans and made it possible to consider offensive operations for 1918. However, it would not be Sarrail who would be in charge as his military failures and meddling in Greek political affairs led to his replacement by Gen Guillaumat in December 1917.

For the troops 'up country', Christmas 1917 once again proved to be a generally quiet affair, with Briton and Bulgar again respecting each other's holidays. As comforts were generally lacking, commanders tried to make an effort over the Christmas period to make the lives of their troops more enjoyable:

This is the one day in the year when the Army really lets its hair down and tries to make our miserable lives happy! To start with, we get decent grub – bacon and tomatoes for breakfast for a kick off. The weather is perfect and, for once, Johnny behaves himself and does not annoy us whilst our own guns also kept quiet . . . After a voluntary Church Parade which lasted exactly 21 minutes (I timed it!) we have more football before the piece de resistance of the day – our Christmas dinner. This turns out to be a real Lucullan feast, consisting of roast turkey or roast goose, with all the fillings, or roast beef, spuds and greens with liberal helpings of 'pudden' to follow, so we all do ourselves remarkably well. Free beer is also provided and we finish off with cigarettes, cigars and oranges. We were apparently not too full up to enjoy a 'comic' football match in the afternoon between the 'old crocks', which was great fun, and then back to a very satisfying tea of pears, milk and rock cakes, with coffee and rum in the evening. The whole far exceeds our expectations and proves miles ahead of the proverbial 'Christmas Day in the Workhouse'.[8] (*Pte William Denton Mather, 8th Ox & Bucks Light Infantry*)

This was done despite the ravages to shipping in the Mediterranean caused by German and Austro-Hungarian U-boats, which accounted for

Men of a British field artillery battery with assorted fresh meat for their Christmas dinner, Cidemli Ravine, Doiran-Vardar sector, Salonika Front, 1917. *(Private collection)*

the non-arrival of much mail and gifts from home as well as official supplies. Where possible, trading was done with local villagers for rabbits, turkeys, geese, hens and even goats. Some enterprising soldiers even tried rearing their own livestock or poultry. One of these was Pte Fred Warburton, serving with an ammunition column in the village of Gugunci behind the Doiran Front:

One of the drivers had some months before discovered some nests with 5 goslings in so it had been decided that we would rear them for Xmas. There was an old church without a roof in our compound so I made shelters and with a bit of care we got them on their feet. I may tell you we were very jealous of those geese and as we saw them grow we would do voluntary guard . . . the week before Christmas I weighed them and they were over 15lb gross each so we worked it out that we would have over 2lb of goose each as there was only 22 of us including the officers and we had decided to give them one for themselves.

I should explain that while our camp was on a hillside on the other side over the nullah and facing us was a forward unit of the RAMC.

Christmas Eve and we had arranged for a two hour spell to watch the geese and Dick Best had relieved for the 4 to 6 after which we would all be up, our cook Reg usually got up before that time to make gunfire, all of a sudden we heard Reg shouting so we all hurried out to find Dick fast asleep in the corner of the old church, we tried to waken him but it seemed impossible, at his side was a water bottle still quarter full of rum and all we could identify was RAMC in indelible ink and there were NO geese so our Xmas dinner had vanished and all we had left was a tin of Daily Mail pudding. Although we could smell them cooking they, the Medics, said they had bought them, it took us all our time to stop a free for all but as usual the Rob-All-My-Comrades won.

Some of the more remote detachments, such as the anti-aircraft gun section on the Aegean island of Thasos, appear to have been forgotten by the authorities and were in no position to forage for themselves:

Dec 25th. Tuesday. Christmas Day. As I thought we had a splendid dinner of bully beef and preserved potatoes our usual fare. I think I have tasted roast beef once since last June, we seem to be forgotten for everything on this fever stricken island, while at Headquarters at Mudros they live on the fat of the land. (*Sgt Howard Couldrake, 3rd Royal Marine Light Infantry*)

The resentment felt by Couldrake towards those in the rear areas was common in Macedonia as even officers had but limited chances to visit the bright lights of Salonika. This created a real division between the front-line soldiers and those they nicknamed 'Base Wallahs'. Such differences were very apparent at Christmas time:

Well, here Xmas is over, and also my birthday; nothing very exciting. On Xmas Eve we had a very good concert party here and a lot of people including my Colonel. I had asked the General up but he was unable to come, for which I was devoutly thankful when the time came, as he is always late and we had very little time for dinner, as it was. There were a lot of fair sisters from a neighbouring hospital, and altogether our mess was crammed to suffocation. All my men celebrated freely and several of my old Irish P.B. policemen set to and had a fierce encounter, several being laid out. Xmas day I went to church in the morning; in the afternoon we had a footer match and in the evening the men sat down to their Xmas dinner at 6pm and we at 7pm. I had to go round and make speeches, read messages from the G.O.C. etc. The men had a terrific dinner and Heaven knows how much they drank. They follow up by what they called a free and easy which consisted of more liquors and doing as much damage as possible. However there was no serious trouble so I got off easy; one gent however was carted off to hospital 36 hours after, still unconscious; presumably he had a bad fall when tight. We, the officers, had a very quiet evening. Boxing day, my birthday, was like any other day, except I had to stand drinks all round . . .

We have a concert tonight and some Australian sisters coming; they have an awful Cockney twang, and don't look half so smart as the Canadians.[9] (*2/Lt Eric de Normann, ASC*)

The presence of nurses was taken full advantage of, as the chances of seeing an 'English' woman were few and far between in the Balkans:

Today – Christmas Day – was gloriously sunny and very warm. The men organized games and apparently enjoyed themselves immensely. Their midday dinner was a great affair of roast fresh beef (the first I had seen since I arrived in Macedonia) roast potatoes, Christmas pudding, oranges and nuts with beer ad lib. The officers dined at 8 with 'Sister' guests from the Australian Hospital. None was startlingly attractive but they added to the gaiety of the function. We cleared a space in the middle of the Mess after dinner and danced as best we could according to our individual condition of sobriety, or flirted furtively with the 'possibles' but the lynx eyed matron kept her charges well under supervision – quite unnecessarily for nothing but advanced intoxication of the officers could have imperilled the virtue of those Sisters. We finally packed off our guests in motor lorries, kissed them goodbye, and went to bed ourselves. Altogether a wonderful Christmas Day. (*Capt Alfred Bundy, Middlesex Regiment, attached BSF Base Training Camp*)

For troops up the line their best way to escape the trials of campaigning, if only for a short time, was a visit to one of the divisional theatres, which had been established relatively early in the campaign. At the 26th Division's Gaiety Theatre at Kalinova, behind the Doiran Front, Christmas 1917 saw the staging of the pantomime *Robinson Crusoe*:

The show consisted of four acts, preceded by a prologue, and four complete changes of costume. The first act; leaving England, the second act; on board ship, the third; in 'Muckidonia' and the fourth; in the palace of Dorian [*sic*]. We had a good strong chorus and the orchestra was good. The place was packed and Weston as Mrs Crusoe made the house rock with laughter.

The only hitch I remember was when the mast of the ship fell in the second act (it was supposed to fall when the ship was torpedoed). It fell on the principal boy's head and made his teeth chatter a bit, but he was able to carry on.

One incident I must put in was a remark made one night by one of the audience. One of the lines the principal boy had to say was 'But I want to be a soldier'. A very fed up voice came from a member of an infantry battalion 'Do yer, well there's a blighter here whose place you can have.'

Our show soon became famous through the Division. The place was full every night and we gave matinees on Wednesday and Saturday. Men could come down from the line, see the show and be back before morning. (*Pte George Veasey, 8th Ox & Bucks Light Infantry*)

If things were quiet on both sides of the Adriatic the same could not be said for the Middle East. Following unsuccessful attempts to take the town of Gaza in March and April, Gen Sir Edmund Allenby replaced Gen Murray as commander of the Egyptian Expeditionary Force (EEF) on 27 June. After building up his forces, Allenby launched the Third Battle of Gaza (31 October–7 November). This proved a complete success and

Crowds gathered to watch the Christmas procession to the Church of the Nativity in Bethlehem, Christmas Day 1917. The capture of Jerusalem and Bethlehem close to Christmas 1917 may have inspired those at home but, to the troops in Palestine, things could appear somewhat different: *'I am afraid not many of us felt like Gallant Christian Soldiers after wresting Jerusalem from the Infidel after Thousands of Years. The spirit of the Crusaders was conspicuous by its absence . . . The fighting had been bitter and many of our friends were no longer with us . . .' (Gnr Thomas Edgerton, D Battery, 301 Brigade, RFA) (Q 33892)*

steady progress was maintained towards Jerusalem despite tough Turkish resistance. The surrender of Jerusalem on 9 December and Allenby's formal entry into the city two days later fulfilled Lloyd George's request that the city be delivered as a Christmas present for the British people, who had had little in the way of striking victories to celebrate in 1917. This is not to say that the Turks had given up the fight and, as Christmas approached, troops of the EEF found themselves north of Jerusalem covering the Nablus road and waiting for a counter-attack:

On December 23rd we went back into action. We passed through Jerusalem again at night. We take up our position about four miles outside the city astride the Nablus Road. It commences to rain hard. We hear that the Turkish counter attack is imminent. During the 24th we did our best in the appalling weather to dig ourselves in. Christmas Day dawned and the rain came down incessantly. About midday the General in charge of our Division inspected our position with the C.R.A. He did not like it at all and ordered us out. We were, he said, too vulnerable. We were to take up a position some eight hundred yards further back. The rain persisted with a piercing cold wind. Those six guns had to be man-handled out of the mud and on to the road before the teams could hook up and take them away . . . drenched to the skin, cold, and almost exhausted our guns were eventually in position and we looked on in vain for a dry spot to rest. Somebody, somehow managed to brew some tea. The C.O. ordered a rum ration. Hot tea laced with a small dose of rum and bully beef and biscuits was very welcome Christmas fare. Nobody was in festive

British troops fill their water bottles from a canvas trough set up in a Palestinian village, December 1917. *(Q 12888)*

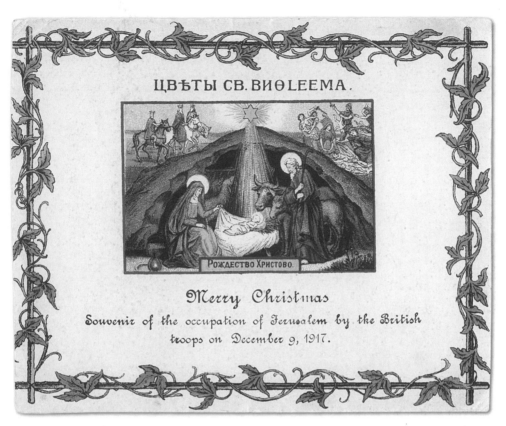

Christmas card produced as a souvenir of the occupation of Jerusalem by British forces on 9 December 1917. *(MISC 74/1113)*

mood. In fact I am quite sure nobody realized what the date was until afterwards. We waited throughout the night for the expected attack but it never came. The rain persisted. I am sure that was the longest, coldest and most miserable night I have ever had. Dawn came and still no attack. Fortunately the rain ceased on the 26th and we were able to sort things out and get a semblance of a gun position. The climax came just before dawn on 27th after heavy bombardment during the night. I don't think we were ever so glad to go into action as we were that night. The suspense had been severe. (*Gnr Thomas Edgerton, D Battery, 301 Brigade, RFA*)

Through the deteriorating weather conditions most men relied on bivouac tents for shelter. The 2/15th Londons, who had been in Salonika the year before, found themselves in the support line near Bire also waiting for the Turkish attack:

Xmas Eve. Such rotten luck, we came out of our billets at midday and relieved the 20th London Regiment at our old place in the line.

The weather was frightful, cold and continuous rain. As soon as we arrived at our position we were detailed to go on a carrying party to 'C' Company who were up in the line. The job was carrying . . . fresh water . . . in a galvanised flat-sided tank taking 12 gallons of water. It was a terrible job slipping and sliding in all the rain and mud, manhandling the heavy tanks. Before going Hewer and I and all others put up their bivouacs hoping to get some shelter from the weather. A Xmas ration of cigarettes was issued.

On the way back from the line we lost our way and finally arrived back at our bivouac at midnight only to find it blown down and under water. The cigarettes were spoilt by the rain. Our camp was in an old quarry, selected for safety from bullets. In the rain it was the worst possible site and just collected water.

I don't think I have ever felt so despondent. After a ration of rum Hewer and I got out of the quarry on to a high slab of stone where we felt safe from being drowned and huddled together to keep as warm as possible. Both of us felt we were bound to die of exposure. What an Xmas Eve. (*Pte Francis Blunt*)

Christmas Day itself proved little better:

Xmas Day dawned at last and with the daylight things looked better. Hewer and I stretched ourselves to confirm that we were still alive and our limbs in working order. The lads moved about and soon some sort of order came. Rations were almost non-existent. We only had one cup of tea all day. At midday we packed up and moved about half a mile further on. At night we went out on outpost duty on a hill called 'White Scar Hill'. Another awful night. Rained continuously. Mud stuck half way up our puttees. When you sat down you could not get up without assistance. What an Xmas Day! How we shall all remember it. (*Pte Francis Blunt*)

Elsewhere troops in the front line were engaged in consolidating positions recently won from the Turks:

On the 23rd we gave the Turks such a bad time that they absolutely cleared off and allowed us to move forward to a new position without resistance. This meant that we were hard at work on the 24th and 25th consolidating the new line. We spent the whole of the night of the 24th building sangers, wiring etc and did the same on Christmas night. These had to be built owing to the fact that in that part of the line it is impossible to dig trenches owing to the rocks.

We should not have minded a bit had it been fine, but it started to rain on the 23rd and continued steadily till the 26th. We all got wet through of course on the first day and had to remain wet till the sun came out again to dry us. When I woke on Christmas morning I found that I was lying in 6" of water and we spent the whole day trying to get warm. In spite of the weather we managed quite a good dinner which made us quite cheery. We got a fresh meat ration of Australian Rabbits which made an excellent stew – then we followed this up with plum pudding and cheese. The plum pudding was a great stroke of luck. Colonel Clutterbuck sent us two from Cairo and the Coys drew for them. I was lucky enough to draw the largest so we had quite a good share each. We also had a ripping cake which Colonel Waddy sent us from India and we ate this sitting round the fire after we had finished work at night.

The parcel mail was the cause of great excitement. There were quite a lot of parcels from home but not the ones intended for Christmas. Those received should have arrived weeks ago. I was lucky enough to receive two from Port Said containing chocolates etc. I ordered them ages ago and had quite given them up for lost and it was a great stroke of luck getting them on Christmas day.

Our Regt was relieved from the line on Boxing Day and I can assure you we were glad enough to march back especially as it was a nice fine sunny day. It is only when you are absolutely wet through and chilled to the bone that you realise what a godsend the sun is.[10] (*Capt James Mackie, 2/4th Somerset Light Infantry*)

On the day the Somersets were relieved, three Turkish divisions launched a determined assault down the line of the Nablus road towards Jerusalem. After heavy fighting their advance was halted and soon afterwards they were put into full retreat. By the end of December the Turks were pushed back into difficult rocky country well north of Jerusalem.

For those wounded during the drive to Jerusalem or suffering from sickness, the various hospitals and field ambulances tried their best to provide a memorable Christmas. However, the procuring of large stocks of fresh meat was often a difficult task as members of the 1/2nd East Anglian Field Ambulance based at Ludd, north of Ramleh, discovered:

December 23 1917: A committee consisting of Robert [Mason], 3 N.C.O.s and myself was appointed by the C.O. to see what could be done. We drew up a list of things, which we would *try* to get from the Canteen, and we decided to *try* to get enough chickens for all the men. Well, the Canteen is 30 miles away and 80–100 chickens would be required. I need hardly say more. Robert consulted the Administrative Commandant of the place, a Maj Ellery, and he arranged that we should get the chickens through the native 'mukta'. I don't know how to spell that word but it sounds something like that. The town is divided into districts and over each district is a mukta whose business seems to be to know exactly what every man in his district has . . .

We then proceeded round this man's district. He would knock at the door, which was generally half open. The door would then be carefully closed and he would shout while a woman screamed from within. A certain amount of wrangling would then ensue, and after 5–10 minutes a fluttering of wings would be heard and then a small child would emerge with a chicken held by the legs . . . The mukta was accompanied by a clerk who wrote down the name of the vendor and the price – the money was to be paid by the Administrative Committee the next morning. After buying about 12–20 Robert and I got tired of it and withdrew, sending the Sgt-Maj and a Sgt to take our place. We got over 30 chickens that afternoon altogether and we had to make an enclosure for them – this we did by digging a big square hole in the ground and covering it with a tarpaulin. (*Maj E.B. Hinde*)

Such efforts were well received by the patients, not only helping them to forget for a while their wounds or illness, but for some a wish to join in with the festive entertainments gave renewed strength and worked towards speeding their recovery. This may have been particularly true of those who tried to remain with their unit rather than be evacuated for medical care:

Xmas Day: Awoke feeling ever so much better but I don't suppose that I shall be able to get up. A communion service is held at 7am taken by a minister, who is a corporal in 423 (S) Bty. Then breakfast at 8am consisting of coffee and Quaker oatcakes, then tea, bread and butter, ham and eggs. A church parade at 10am where a few more carols were sung. Dinner was served up at 1 o'clock. All the officers were down and a large marquee had been erected with seats and tables for everybody and a platform at one end. The OC made a very nice speech in which he said that he hoped that we should all be together next year in the event of the war extending so long and if anything did separate us it would be that we were each at our respective homes. A few toasts were drunk and then dinner. First course was roast beef, potatoes, beans etc, then real plum duff with sauce and after that beer, spirits, mineral water, nuts, oranges, sweets, cigars and cigarettes.

I have some real good pals in this bivvi and they looked after me a treat. I had everything brought that I wanted and nearly everybody in the battery came to see how I was getting on, and sympathysed with me. I was close to the marquee and could hear all that was going on. After dinner I got up and dressed. I assured the medical orderly that I felt pretty fair, and I went to tea, which consisted of tea, bread, butter and jam. The bread we get is good white bread and the butter was the ordinary Danish. I wish that everybody in England had such a feed as we had. The officers are quite good and the Quarter Master is one of the best. As I have said on many occasions this battery is next to none. I daresay that every day we live better than thousands do in England. The only thing to spoil the days proceedings was that we had occasional heavy showers, and in the evening vivid lightning and thunder, but this didn't prevent us enjoying ourselves. At 7.30 we had a real fine concert given by officers and men of the battery. At the interval we have refreshments in the shape of beer etc, biscuits and cheese (not army biscuits). I was present at the concert so I did not do bad after all. I still kept fairly well. I might say that this is the same position as we occupied previous to the battle for Gaza, so roughly speaking we are about 80 miles behind the firing line. We haven't fired a shot for seven weeks. There was nothing to spoil our Christmas only orders to move and these never came. We often thought about those at home and wondered what kind of a time they were having. If everybody did as well as we did they wouldn't do bad. It was a great improvement on last Christmas which I spent in Salonika, and I hope to further improve next year by all of us being at home. (*Gnr Ernest Hinchcliffe, RGA*)

Jerusalem was not the only famous city of the Middle East to be captured by British forces during 1917, as on 11 March, troops under Maj-Gen Maude had entered Baghdad in Mesopotamia. The capture of this fabled city was a great morale boost to the Allied cause, being the first major victory, in any theatre of war, after the very tough and generally inconclusive fighting of 1916. In just three months Maude had steadily advanced his force up the line of the Tigris, prising the Turks out of a number of tough positions and taking Kut-al-Amara on 24 February. Although offensive operations continued after the fall of Baghdad, there was to be no decisive end to the campaign in 1917. Indeed, the gloss was rather taken off the year's successes by the death of Maude from cholera on 18 November. Operations were then halted for the winter by his successor, Lt Gen Sir William Marshall, leaving most of the troops to celebrate a quiet Christmas in tented camps as the Turks tried to reorganise their forces for the defence of Mosul in northern Mesopotamia:

Just a line while I have the opportunity and before I freeze to death. Alas the cold weather and winds are on us morn and night with heat in between. Yesterday I had two and a half inches of ice in my bucket and a bitter wind . . .

As you know, our successful operations are over for the present or at least there is a slight lull. There are going to be lots of sports down the

Officers' lines and Mess marquees in the camp occupied by the 1st Connaught Rangers between December 1917 and March 1918. The camp was located on the right bank of the River Tigris. Such camps formed the standard type of accommodation for troops in Mesopotamia when not in the front line. *(Q 49775)*

line at Baghdad this Xmas. I am one of the Regt team for the football tournament and we are doing four to five hours training per day. We are also sending four boxers and hope to leave this awful spot in the wilderness on 20th. There will be a certain percentage from each Corps down there.[11] (*Capt Conrad Price, 2nd Norfolks*)

Baghdad was also a focus for the troops' attention as mail from home passed through the city on its way to be distributed amongst the various units:

We have heard that the long over due mail was to reach Baghdad on the 22nd so we hope to get the letters, at all events, just about Xmas, even if we have to wait a bit for the parcels. It has been dreadful going for over three weeks without news of you. I wonder if this is the 'Xmas mail' or if that is not due to come till February, as usual. I wonder too if an intermediate mail has been sunk.[12] (*Capt Charles Baxter, 6th South Lancashires*)

Christmas card sent to Mr and Mrs Smith of Barnsley by a member of the 15th Division from the Falluja area of Mesopotamia on 15 November 1917. This was one of a series of cards printed and published by The Times Press in Bombay. Each card had a different view of Mesopotamia. (*Private collection*)

Luckily, Baxter and his comrades did not have too much longer to wait for their mail:

On the evening of the 26th the Christmas mail did eventually arrive. It was about a month's mail too, so I got an enormous haul. Eight letters from you and three from Eric and a few others . . .

Thank you very much too for the photographs of the garden in winter and summer, which arrived in the third letter. The Yucca must be perfectly lovely when it is in full bloom. I suppose the colour of the flowers is white, isn't it? The sight of the snow makes one feel positively cold! It is very nice to see all the trees and lawns and everything again, as I have seen very little of that sort of thing since leaving England.[13] (*Capt Charles Baxter*)

Such comments show the great importance of letters and other reminders of home, especially to troops serving in such an alien environment as Mesopotamia. Additionally the mail brought gifts from home and these, along with items from Expeditionary Force canteens and company stores, helped cheer the men's desert Christmas:

Christmas Day – Tuesday: Come off guard at 6am and have a holiday spending the time between meals at football. We do pretty well for food issue rations being for breakfast small rashers of bacon, portion of tinned kippers and ¼ tin of machonicie. Lunch rice and fruit, dinner stew and about 1oz of pudding which had been sent from Blighty by some fund in Acton.

Beside this I had bought from the Company Stores 1 tin of salmon, 2 tins of Sardines, 1 tin of Cocoa and 3 packets of biscuits, we also had rum issue at night. So we had a fairly good time. (*L/Cpl W.C. Gale, 2nd Norfolks*)

Even those not able to get down to Baghdad for the sports, or on some other pretext, were able to tell their families at home that they had spent a good Christmas, albeit under campaigning conditions:

Ours was not so bad at all in fact I think it was as nice as it could possibly have been under the circumstances.

The weather, which is the main thing, was perfect. Sunshine and no wind, and the hottest day we have had for a long time, and of course that made all the difference.

The C.O., Tiny and Birch came round in the morning, and Charlton made a speech to my company (which as you know, is over a mile away out in the blue). He did not speak for very long, but just told them what fine fellows they were, as indeed they are, and reminded them of Xmas in the past, when he or Birch commanded the company and wished them a merry Xmas and many merrier ones in England in the future. Then I called for three cheers for the C.O. and dismissed the parade and entertained our three guests for quite a long time.

A two days sports programme had been arranged. It was to be more or less of a comic show, with none of the usual items. However the first event – the only event of the morning – was a serious thing. It was a three miles cross country race, competed for by companies and everybody was all out to win it. I was delighted with the result, as my company won it, more or less in a walkover, somewhat to everybody else's surprise, though not to my own. We got five places out of the first ten men in, which was far better than even I had expected.

In the afternoon too, we were very successful, but there was nothing that I cared about winning so much as the race of the morning.

The men didn't do so badly in the food line . . . Every man had a parcel and about 6 oz of plum pudding from the 'Ladies of India' and we officers all contributed towards providing them with a bottle each of Japanese beer – a somewhat expensive but very satisfactory item. The Government as usual, did not provide a single thing in the way of extra food. Perhaps however it was all snaffled by the S & T.

As for the officers, we were extraordinarily lucky, as one of our convoys had been down . . . to bring up stores from the Expeditionary Force Canteen . . . and had been held up by rain. However it reached us on Xmas eve, and just saved us from an almost 'ration' Xmas. You see no mail has arrived for nearly a month. Even as it was we had to share the men's plum pudding, not having any of our own (We always leave anything in the way of gifts or free luxuries of any sort to the men, except in very special circumstances). But we had a real goose for dinner, not a tinned variety either, and had lots of other good foods.

Some of the other companies had turkeys but we drew for them and we failed in as much as we drew a goose. But there was really more on it than on some of the turkeys, which were rather small.[14] (*Capt Charles Baxter*)

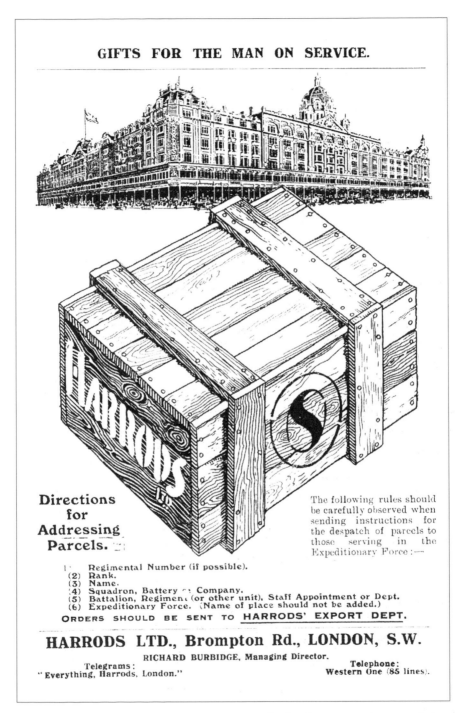

GIFTS FOR THE MAN ON SERVICE.

Directions for Addressing Parcels.

The following rules should be carefully observed when sending instructions for the despatch of parcels to those serving in the Expeditionary Force:—

(1) Regimental Number (if possible).
(2) Rank.
(3) Name.
(4) Squadron, Battery or Company.
(5) Battalion, Regiment (or other unit), Staff Appointment or Dept.
(6) Expeditionary Force. (Name of place should not be added.)

ORDERS SHOULD BE SENT TO **HARRODS' EXPORT DEPT.**

HARRODS LTD., Brompton Rd., LONDON, S.W.

RICHARD BURBIDGE, Managing Director.

Telegrams:
"Everything, Harrods, London."

Telephone:
Western One (85 lines).

Page from the 1917 Harrods catalogue *Gifts for the Man on Service*, giving directions on how to address a parcel to ensure it reached soldiers serving overseas. *(Harrods Archive)*

Like troops in Mesopotamia, those chasing the elusive von Lettow-Vorbeck around East Africa were also enjoying a lull in the fighting. This was because the Germans had slipped into Portuguese territory on 25 November, which signalled the failure of British forces, under Gen van Deventer, to prevent such a move. The Schutztruppe now numbered only some 300 Germans and 1,700 Askaris. But these were the fittest men von Lettow-Vorbeck had and for the remainder of the campaign he would rely on mobility rather than fighting strength as his chief weapon. During December the Germans re-equipped with weapons and ammunition by raiding Portuguese garrisons, the latter's forces being too weak and disorganised to prevent this. At the same time British forces did little to assist their ally and were content to patrol the frontier, increase their hold on German East Africa and ready their forces for a new campaigning season. To prepare for this, new recruits to the King's African Rifles were put through their paces at training camps such as that at M'bagathi, 12 miles west of Nairobi. Here Lt J. Elliott (3rd/6th KAR), the machine-gun training officer, had a more eventful Christmas than he anticipated:

Xmas 1917 and New Year 1918 were great celebrations. We did a bit of riding, running down the zebras which were in thousands near us, a bit of shooting getting a buck or two, and spent the nights trying to sleep in the heat. One night I had dozed off when I was awakened by the feeling that I was being struck by thousands of red-hot needles. I lit my lamp and jumped out into the open for the banda and every inch of me, bed and everything was a moving mass of red 'safari' ants . . .

Hell! I broke open the Q.M. Stores and slept under the stars that night, and I was a mass of minute red punctures the next morning, but the ants had moved on and the Mess had a good laugh at me . . .

The Governor General dined with us one night, and as there were nine Scots in the Mess the G.G. suggested an eightsome reel, and, of course, a request from him was an order. One got the pipes skirling and the other eight of us danced the reel on the mud floor with the temperature over 90 degrees in the hut. The dust rose in clouds and I can remember the G.G. standing in the anteroom hut with field glasses fixed to his eyes trying to see us through the dust.

Of course, the campaign in East Africa, like those in Mesopotamia and Salonika, witnessed many more casualties caused by disease than by enemy action. As far as possible the worst cases were taken out of theatre by hospital ship. Many of these men would spend Christmas 1917 in South African hospitals, such as No. 3 General Hospital at Durban:

Christmas Day was rather dull – just an extra good dinner and nothing more – except for a few evergreens and flags scattered about the ward. I always thought Xmas in hospital was one long orgie of merriment and was rather disappointed. We had a few small gifts from the Durbanites, of which the most useful was 10/- each from the Turf Club. There was considerably more excitement on the 27th when the tent I was in consisting of three marquees joined together, and containing about 30 patients caught fire about one o'clock in the morning and in about ten minutes was burnt to the ground. Nobody was hurt, but the difficulty was to find accommodation for us, the hospital being very full; and we sat around in a lettuce patch in pyjamas and slippers while they discussed the situation. For me they found a very comfortable bed in the Sgt. Majs tent, but most then had to share the few mattresses that were rescued from the fire on the floor of the mess tent, a hard bed but perhaps better than a bed of lettuces. The next day they scattered us among various wards. I am now in what was a drill hall . . .

The people I met at Durban last time have been to see me and I have not wanted for cigarettes, fruit and literature. Since I have begun to get about a bit I have been to see them and had some whiskey and soda and been for a very decent motor ride.[15] (*Sgt Roland Mountfort, 25th Royal Fusiliers*)

Peace at Last! Christmas 1918

I wish to remind all ranks serving under my command that during the trying and unavoidably extended period that must elapse before the demobilization of the Egyptian Expeditionary Force can be expected, the good name of the British Army depends upon the individual conduct of each member of the Force in the various countries now in our occupation.

Courtesy and consideration to the inhabitants of these countries were never more essential, even during the period of active operations, than they are now, and I feel certain that I can rely on every member of this Force to maintain the traditions of the British Army in this respect.

In these countries special temptations exists with regard to Wine and Women. Both must be resisted. Our relatives and friends are anxiously awaiting our return home, and they will expect to find all those of us who have escaped wounds in action with our physical and our moral energies unimpaired. Treat all women with courtesy, but shun all undue intimacy. Remember that temptation, which when encountered is hard to resist, is often easy to avoid.

Final impressions are usually the more lasting; and on the behaviour of the troops during the present period will depend the final impression left by the British Army on the inhabitants of these countries.

The honour of the Egyptian Expeditionary Force is in your hands. I do not fear to leave it there.

General Sir Edmund Allenby's Special Order of the Day, January 1919

For troops celebrating Christmas in 1918, the wishes for peace expressed by them and their comrades over the previous four years had finally come true. When the guns fell silent on the Western Front at 11 a.m. on 11 November, victory for the Allies was complete. The process began in the Balkans with the Bulgarians signing an armistice on 30 September, followed within weeks by the Turks (30 October) and Austria-Hungary (4 November).

This final march to victory had been a hard-fought struggle with the British and French having weathered a series of German offensives between 21 March and 15 July. The German gamble was played in an attempt to win the war before American manpower made itself felt on the Western Front. Transferring 23 Divisions from Russia, Ludendorff achieved a superior concentration of manpower for his offensive. However, he was forced to leave over one million German and Austro-Hungarian troops in the East to further German territorial ambitions in the chaos of Bolshevik Russia. Ludendorff's first blow fell on the weakened British 5th Army who were thrown into confusion by the speed of the German assault. In a pattern that played itself out in each of the major German attacks of 1918, an initial successful breakthrough and advance was gradually checked by a combination of stiffening resistance by Allied forces, tiredness among the German infantry and the inability of their artillery and logistic support to keep pace with the advance. When the Germans were halted by French troops on the Marne in July, Ludendorff's war-winning strategy was in ruins and his army no longer had any reserves of manpower to make good their heavy losses.

When the Allies went over to the offensive in August, the lead role was played by Haig's forces. Despite suffering a manpower shortage brought on by the heavy losses of late 1917 and having large numbers of men deployed in other theatres of war, British, Dominion and Empire troops, supported by the French and Americans, went on to defeat the German field army in 100 days of offensive action, including the storming of the strong Hindenburg Line position.

Not unexpectedly, with the fighting having finished on 11 November, many of Britain's citizen soldiers wondered why they were still in uniform come Christmas. Such thoughts led to a growing resentment against military discipline as many viewed themselves as civilians once again:

Strangely enough now that the war is over, numbers of the men refuse to obey orders or rather they show a certain amount of independence

Christmas card produced by the XIX Corps in 1918, showing the Old Belfry, Courtrai, where the Corps was located during the winter of 1918–19. This particular card was sent home on 21 December 1918 by a member of 173 Field Company (RE) with the following message: *'My Dear Kaye, My best wishes to you in every way go with this. I hope you are home and free from anything military now and beginning to look around. Write and let me know all your doings and how you are keeping. We are hoping to become "Ship" men pretty soon. All send best wishes to you, Sincerely, John.'* (A.E. Kaye collection 82/11/1)

that is most disconcerting. I had to talk to a whole company that were disgracefully abusive to their officers. I realized that any show of military authority would be fatal so I reasoned with them and told them that for the benefit of all and in order to facilitate the movement of those who were anxious to get back to England, it was necessary that they should still behave as disciplined soldiers. My remarks were greeted by cat calls and rude noises but I knew there must be a large proportion of the men who were anxious to return to England, so I announced that I should look to the men themselves for co-operation and that if there was obstruction I should have the offenders arrested and kept back. There was then almost complete silence and I had no further difficulty. (*Capt Alfred Bundy, 2nd King's Own Royal Lancasters*)

The men referred to by Bundy were at Summerhill Camp outside Salonika, where soldiers not wanted for occupation forces in Bulgaria and Turkey had been kicking their heels since the end of September. But lapses in discipline were not confined to more distant theatres of war or to other ranks:

> I think I will be a bit fond of staying in when I do come home. No Germany for me, thank you; I've seen quite enough of Germans. And I will be so pleased to say good-byeee to muddy Flanders . . .
>
> There was a parade on Boxing Day. Two others and myself thought it was a holiday and no parade. So we did not go. Result is we do three extra parades beginning Monday, with full marching order on, after the others are dismissed. What a cheerful army. They would have had us on parade Xmas day if they could. Oh I aint arf enjoying myself. If leave continues, I think my turn comes about Feb to March. And I sincerely hope that its home for good . . . I hope you enjoyed your Xmas and had a real good time. No need to worry now, war's over,

Two officers of the 95th Russel's Infantry outside a tent in the officers' lines in the regiment's snow-covered camp between Kilkis and Yanesh in Macedonia, December 1918. *(2003-03-02)*

so they say. We painted all our limbers and cleaned guns etc ready for handing in – sometime.[1] (*Lt Emrys Richards, 63rd Battalion, MGC*)

Unfortunately, the initial demobilisation scheme, drawn up in 1917 by the Secretary of State for War Lord Derby, proposed that the first men to be released from service were those who worked in key industries. However, it was invariably these men who had been called up in the latter stages of the war. This left many of those with the longest service records at the back of the queue, which was the main cause of resentment. Soldiers from the Dominions also suffered delays, many waiting months in camps in Britain for transport home. Once Churchill was appointed Secretary of State for War in January 1919, he amended the demobilisation programme, making sure that age, length of service and wounds were taken into account when selecting the order in which men were sent home. But until then the authorities worried about unrest in the ranks

Christmas card produced by BEF General Headquarters, France, 1918. (*Capt P.M. Sharp collection 78/69/1*)

Christmas card produced by 33 Casualty Clearing Station, France, 1918. *(Canon R.L. Hussey collection P 452)*

as small-scale mutinies broke out in Calais and Folkestone and a demonstration of 3,000 soldiers occurred in central London. Typical of the men they were trying to appease was Gnr William Young (175 Siege Battery, RGA), who wrote to his fiancée from the village of Villers-Bocage:

We are expecting to move at any time to another village near here. They have been putting up huts for us for some time now and they are about ready I think. So they shouldn't be so bad but it will be a good job when we can get out of it. It gets on your nerves to be messing about doing nothing when you might be at home. They have started issuing us out with a rifle now the war is over, I suppose they think we want something to look after now the fighting is over. They didn't give us one when that was on, but I suppose that's just like the Army. I don't know what I want that for, but still it don't matter, shall stand it in the

Christmas card produced by the Royal Engineers CME (Light Railway) Workshops in France, 1918, showing Kaiser Wilhelm II being knocked over by a British light railway locomotive. (*Canon R.L. Hussey collection P 452*)

corner out of the way. I have been on exchange work since being here so haven't had to do any parades, so that is one thing to be thankful for.[2]

Across the various former theatres of war, officers and NCOs worked hard to provide for their men in preparation for what most realised would be their final Christmas together:

25 December 1918: Maglia:
Christmas Day was celebrated in a fashion wholly British in this small Italian village, and despite inclement weather, the arrangements made by the Battalion went off splendidly. In the morning the officers played the sergeants at football and the former were rather heavily beaten 7–3. The match however provided a good deal of fun, as the ground was in a very bad condition in many places completely under water. At 12.30 the Christmas dinners by Companies began and continued well into

the afternoon. 'A' Coy had their real Christmas dinner the evening before owing to the difficulty in securing a room for Christmas Day. Lt-Col Bartlett DSO was unfortunately away, on leave, but when Maj P. PICKFORD DSO, MC visited the dining rooms, he was acclaimed by all ranks and toasted with musical honours, not once but many times. Scenes of joyous hilarity ensued and Christmas Day 1918 was undoubtedly the most enjoyable the Battalion had spent under active service conditions. (*War Diary 1/4th Ox & Bucks Light Infantry*)

As the fighting ceased, there was, in general, more of a loosening of military discipline around the celebrations, especially for those in camps awaiting the end of their military service. Drinking had always been an integral part of the soldier's way of celebrating and many took full advantage of the changed circumstances they found at Christmas 1918:

Xmas Eve. Very gusty weather today and inclined to rain. A General Holiday. Sports which were to have taken place today are postponed to Boxing Day . . .

There was a Fancy Dress Ball in the canteen tonight but it was just spoilt by booze. A lot too much silly drinking; did not appeal to me. I went to bed early, thinking of the children in England 'hanging up their stockings' . . .

Thursday 26 December 1918: The Sports this afternoon were very good, all the usual running and jumping races. In the evening I went down to the Section and packed a box for home. Sgt Pat was absolutely canned [drunk]. (*2 ACM Francis Blunt, 17 Training Depot Squadron, RAF Abu Sueir*)

As 2/Lt Eric de Normann put it: 'Xmas is always rather strenuous in the Army. The eating and drinking is always rather overdone – especially the latter.'[3] At Marsh Pier Supply Depot, outside Salonika, where de Normann found himself that winter, the freely flowing alcohol led to an excess of Christmas spirit on the part of the men who became keen on showing the officers their vocal dexterity:

Men of a Royal Engineer Signal Company plucking turkeys for their dinner on Christmas Day, Italy, 1918. *(Q 26213)*

Last night we were invaded by two bands of carol singers all rather hoarse and unsteady! . . .

Most of the men didn't go to bed last night, consequently everybody is rather tired. I went to bed at eleven, at 2 they had a debate as to whether they should sing carols outside my hut – luckily they decided I might object.[4] (*2/Lt Eric de Normann, ASC*)

This is not to say that Blunt and de Normann did not enjoy the festive season that year. The former found his Christmas Day notably different from that he had experienced with the 2/15th Londons in 1917:

Xmas Day, Beautiful warm sunny day. Turkey, Xmas pudding etc for Xmas Dinner. Dinner supposed to cost 6/- a head but it was certainly not worth it. Excellent football match this afternoon between the staff and the pupils. This evening there was a splendid concert in the

Officers of the 95th Russel's Infantry trying to keep warm in their Mess hut in a camp between Kilkis and Yanesh in Macedonia, December 1918. *(2003-03-02)*

canteen which lasted until after midnight. During the evening Cobb and I took two flashlight photos of the Officers' Mess dinner. They would insist on us joining with the champagne and other drinks. I went to bed at 1.30am tired out after a perfect day – such a contrast to a year ago, in the trenches beyond Jerusalem.

For de Normann, New Year's Eve 1919 also brought first-class entertainment:

We had a great show here last night; the biggest social success of the Balkans! Namely a real pukka dance! Dancing was allowed this year to all sisters, and I had a bevy of Australian girls down – our mess looked awfully pretty. We had decorated it with signal flags – polished the floor – had a fine orchestra – good supper, plenty of champagne and were all as merry as larks from 8.30 till 3. I haven't enjoyed myself so much since I was in the army.[5]

As at military camps, the staff of military hospitals ensured the men in their care would not miss out on the celebrations. Among these was 3rd Air Mechanic John Roscoe (20th Depot Training Squadron), who was in Government Hospital, Suez, suffering from dysentery:

A tree has been fitted up in the yard, and electric lights arranged on it, while every night for the last week I have heard the staff and some of the patients downstairs singing Christmas carols. I suppose they intend to come round as Xmas waits. The music is mostly provided by the gramophone!

Christmas card produced by British forces in Mesopotamia celebrating victory over the Turks in 1918. *(Private collection)*

Cover of the menu card and concert programme of the 10th (Irish) Division Signal Company (RE), Mena Camp, Egypt, Christmas 1918. *(MISC 208/3039)*

Menu and list of performers at the festivities at Mena Camp. *(MISC 208/3039)*

MENA CAMP -- Xmas 1918.

Descriptive Guide to the Mungaree.	Operation Orders for Evening Attack.

C S.M. S. ROSE, R·E. In the Chair.

HORS D'ŒUVRES.

Suvla Oysters whith Shrapnel Sauce.   Whizz-Bangs on Toast.

SOUPS.

Mock Tibbin.   Mud de Picket Line

FISH.

Cod   —   From Lake Balua.

Stew, Airline, Stunt Pattern.

NOTICE :— It is snspected that a one inch cube of meat, lost from the Cook House, may have found its way into this stew. Finder please return

Binte — Arabic. (Certified Disinfected).

Ana muskeeu.   Givit Bucksheesh.

Chicken, Spring, Egyptian.

(This bird was not, as has been stated, found in the Ark, but in the Great Pyramid).

TURKEY.

Left behind at NABLUS ;   Very much Hunderdone.

Camel Cutlets.   (Cuttled by the «Rice»).

Duff, Army style ;   Like Mother used to make.

(Hammers and Jumpers from Massie).

«DESERT»

Eggs - a - Cook.   Sand   Cakes - a - Good.

Biscuits, Jones model, portable, 35 hole.

(Bent biscuits cannot be replaced

without an I.O M's Certificate).

Cheese ????   Gas masks to be worn.

MAFISH.

MITCHELSON will put up an intense Barrage on the Piano, after which the following Artistes (just returned from a successful tour in Palestine) will GO Over The Top :—

ALEFOUNDER.   BROCKLEBANK.   FULTON.   HOLMES.

JOHNSON.   GLOCK.   MARTIN.   ROBERTSON.

RUSSELL.   SCOTT.   WADEY.

During the Battle, the Renowned Juggler, MASSIE, will present his marvellous act of juggling with Beer Bottles and Permanent Poles,

Don't miss WEIGHT, the Conjurer. — See him produce bucksheesh mules from Nowhere.

McKerr will sing that pathetic Ballad, Your Book won't stand it».

The Ration King, SKINNER, will recite that dramatic Poem. «Bring Back that Sack».

As Wartime Christmas Days have passed.
We've hoped that each might be the Last ;
And now the Last has really come
Our eyes are keenly set on Home—
Roll on the day that takes us thére.
When, free from Military Care,
We'll hand our rifles into Store,
And don our «Civvy» clothes once more.

J. G. M.

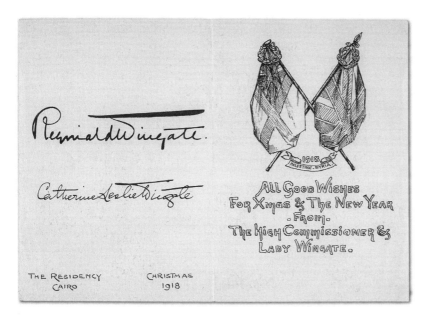

Christmas card sent to troops of the EEF in 1918 by the High Commissioner of Egypt and his wife, Lord and Lady Wingate. *(MISC 38/694)*

I went to the early morning Communion Service today. It was held in an empty ward downstairs. At 7 a.m. we got breakfast. The menu was as follows: Bread & butter, tea, 2 fried eggs, 1½ beef sausages, jam (damson). So you see we did jolly well. Even the patients on the No. 1 diet got the same breakfast, but the poor chaps couldn't quite manage such a lot all at once, and those that ate all their own stuff were far too full up to think of helping anybody else.

The orderly came round first thing this morning with a big sack, from which he extracted small bags containing the patients' Xmas gifts from the Red Cross. In mine I found 5 pkts cigarettes and 2 boxes matches (I gave all these away), a cardboard box of sweets (I did not give these away), a purple handkerchief, soap tablet, towel, writing paper, a Xmas card and a black lead.[6]

The sheer size of the British Army still in the field at the end of 1918, especially in France, meant that not all units could be accommodated in camps. Many continued to be billeted in towns and villages among the civilian population. One such unit was the 63rd Battalion of the Machine Gun Corps, which moved to the village of Elouges on 4 December:

Christmas card produced by the 6th Division in 1918. The card was published by Raphael Tuck & Sons Ltd. *(MISC 38/694)*

Lt Col Graham Seton Hutchinson DSO, MC, officer commanding the 33rd Battalion, MGC, dressed as Father Christmas distributing gifts to French children, 1918. In total Hutchinson visited eighteen villages that Christmas, riding on a captured German wagon pulled by thirty pairs of mules, each pair having a postillion (rider on the left mule). *(Q 56265)*

We were very cordially received by the inhabitants and the Battalion marched past before dispersing to billets.

It was soon evident that with a little organization the Battalion would be very comfortable and it was with that idea that everyone settled down to work. All the men were very comfortable, every man either having bed or palliasse. (*Battalion War Diary*)

The troops quickly settled in and began organising recreation rooms, company dining halls and a battalion Sergeants' Mess and Officers' Mess. Between 9 and 16 December, much time was taken up with cleaning, painting and storing the unit's equipment, including machine guns and limbers. Sports including boxing, football, running and tug-of-war were undertaken in the afternoons to select teams to enter Divisional and Corps level competitions. Preparations were also undertaken to run the army education scheme, for those men wishing to prepare for new careers after demobilisation. This relatively quiet, settled life in the village, with the knowledge that no more fighting was necessary, proved most welcome and a sort of halfway house between the army and the civilian life to which most men longed to return:

Its quite a treat to be in a house, a fire going and sleeping between sheets and two army blankets per man. Although we are not quite free from our numerous friends.[7] (*Lt Emrys Richards*)

Sometimes lice proved not to be the only problem for the troops as life among civilians could have its drawbacks:

19 December 1918: A great deal of commotion was caused by the presence of scabies. This was attributed to civilian sanitation. Although numerous latrines had been erected it was very difficult to ensure that the civilian places were not being used. However careful inspections and a liberal used of creasol soon got rid of the problem. (*63rd Battalion, MGC, War Diary*)

But, on the whole, benefits more than outweighed any inconveniences and discomforts:

Many thanks for parcel received quite safely, also letter dated 19th, everything was quite alright and very nice. It had been a long time in reaching me and the box had got broken a good bit but everything was there alright and in good condition and I thank you so very much for sending me such a nice parcel although I think it must have cost you a lot to send me so many things. I like them all very much it's very kind of you to send them when you are so busy at home. You seem to know exactly what I wanted I think I should have plenty of everything to last until I get home now, I hope so anyway . . . I do so want to see you soon, this messing about here makes you feel more fed up than ever . . .

Well my darling I hope you had as good a time as possible at Xmas. We had a fairly nice time here, rather quiet, but that didn't matter. I made some mince pies for the Boys. Was up all Xmas eve till ½ past 4

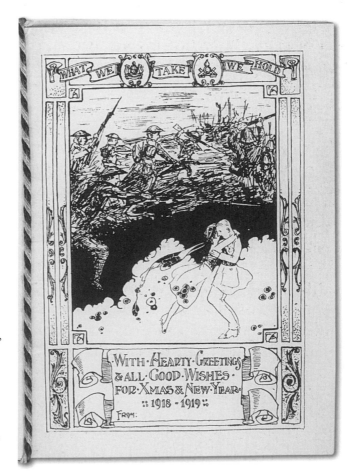

Artwork from the inside of a Christmas card produced by the 96th Infantry Brigade in 1918, showing the contrast between the years of war just fought and the long-awaited return home to loved ones that was soon to come. (*Capt C.E. Leach collection 92/3/1*)

in the morning and then got up and baked the meat for them. We should have had pork, but it was all condemned so it was a good job we didn't get it, we had mutton and some geese, plum pudding and custard. So altogether we had a decent time, only I was a bit tired you may be sure. We had a French bake-house to use and the baker was up with me all night. We didn't have much conversation as neither of us could speak much of the other's language, but we managed to have a few words after a fashion.[8] (*Gnr William Young*)

Many troops once again shared their Christmas celebrations with their civilian hosts, especially in those towns and villages where they had become something of a permanent fixture:

. . . our children's party on the 6th was a great success. They all assembled in the village schoolrooms, it was to begin at 5.30 but at 4.0 they began to arrive! We expected about 120, when I went into the two rooms I counted over 90 in each, and a few more came in later. The Xmas tree was lighted up and we, that is the Officers and Sgts made a procession from the school to the old church (this is our canteen and concert hall etc) it holds about 350 sitting on forms etc. Each of us took a small girl and all the rest of the kids followed on. We walked round the tree and waited, about half the sergeants were in fancy dress, any kind of dress too! Then the adjutant and Green, one of the subalterns, came in dressed as Father Christmas and his wife. Here Father Christmas is not the bringer of toys etc but an old woman called 'Bifara' so our idea worked well. The adjutant made a short speech in Italian, and then began to give away the presents from the tree. We had bought 150 presents and there were about 100 decorations on the tree too. The place was packed, for odd parents had pushed their way in too. The noise was deafening for we had a made-up band of tin trumpets, bugles, drums, any odd things etc and they never ceased. The kids crowded round and I hope everyone got something. Then we took the tree away and gave them cocoa, biscuits, sandwiches of bread and bully beef, cheese and jam, over 1000 were eaten. Then we gave an entertainment of sorts and a dancing bear, elephant, horse, dancers etc all came in and performed and the kids were a bit frightened at first, but they soon got used to them. As they went away, we gave each two oranges and a card. They all really enjoyed themselves and I get smiles from each kid whenever I meet them now![9] (*Lt Col Robert Clarke, 1/4th Royal Berkshires*)

For troops on occupation duty, their relationship with the civilians they came into contact with was more circumspect, as until recently they had been enemies. Additionally, the role of a foreign occupying force is to visibly keep law and order and to enforce a peace settlement on a defeated country. Such a task, when backed up by years of wartime propaganda, painting the enemy in the blackest terms, made the civilian populations of Austria, Bulgaria, Germany and Turkey very wary of the Allied soldiers. In some areas revolutionary activity had led to a near breakdown in law and order and Allied forces drew up plans accordingly.

Men of the 2nd Honourable Artillery Company tobogganing down the hillside road from Landeck, near Imst, Austria, December 1918. '26 Dec – Winter sports in full swing – tobogganing and skiing. Every afternoon spent now in these sports.' (*2nd H.A.C. War Diary*) (Q 26336)

Cast of the pantomime *Sandbag the Sailor*, performed by officers of the 2nd Honourable Artillery Company at Imst, Austria, 31 December 1918. *(Q 26328)*

For example, the 2nd King's Own Royal Lancasters disembarked at Chanak in Turkey on 10 November 1918, having sailed from Salonika three days before. After disabling the guns of various forts in the area they posted companies to forts, road junctions and piers. On 7 December instructions were issued for the defence of Chanak town in the event of civil disturbances. These plans covered both small-scale spontaneous riots and organised political or religious insurrections for which previous warning had been received. In the former situation four platoons, at least 25-men strong and armed with Lewis guns, were to be at the ready. Of these, one platoon would be responsible for guarding the street in which the divisional commander's house was located, while another would move directly to the scene of the disturbance and clear the streets. All other men of the battalion were to stand to arms in their billets on hearing the alarm. In the case of large-scale unrest two full companies were to be sent into the town to hold key points. All roads into Chanak were to be patrolled and all other approaches picqueted. The rest of the battalion were to stand to arms in their billets and await orders. Troops on patrol were to ensure all civilians were confined to their homes and there were strict instructions not to come into conflict with Turkish troops, police or civilians if it could be at all avoided. To reinforce this, machine guns were only to be fired on the order of an officer.

This is not to say that occupying forces always had their hands nervously close to the trigger. The 7th Ox & Bucks Light Infantry moved to the Bulgarian port of Varna on 17 December and soon found themselves mixing freely with the locals. At times, however, their situation appeared rather strange:

The Colonel and Maj Salkeld and I attended a very swagger reception given at the Bulgar Naval and Military Club in honour of ourselves and the French. It struck one as rather ludicrous to see our late enemies standing stiffly to attention when our National Anthem was played. Thanks to Maj Salkeld and Bonner (who had been appointed Foraging Officer) the men had thoroughly good Christmas dinners, with turkeys and geese.

On the 26th December Ker took No. 2 Company over to Balcik (a small town in the Dobrudja on the Black Sea), where they were required to assist in the establishment of the Rumanian civil authorities: this was no easy task, and as was ultimately proved, the whole Battalion was hardly strong enough to carry out this work . . .

The rest of us, in spite of frequent alarms and excitements as to moves in all directions, went on enjoying life in Varna: especially those of us who made friends with Bulgarian families . . .

On New Year's Eve all the officers attended a civic function in our honour; it was a most priceless affair, especially the efforts of some of us to find a language in which to converse with our hosts.[10]
(*Capt A.T.W. Stukeley*)

Even during the advance into Germany some units found ways in which to break the ice with the anxious watching civilians:

On Christmas Eve we stayed in a village schoolroom with some of the bandsmen. There came quite a heavy snowstorm during the evening

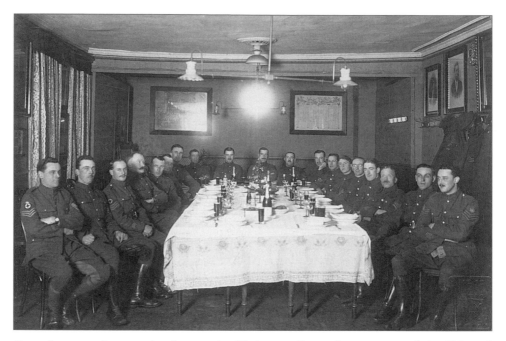

Formal group photograph taken at the Christmas dinner for sergeants of the HQ and No.3 Section of No. 2 Water Tank Company (RE), Cologne, 31 December 1918. *(8008-08)*

with three or four inches of snow. About midnight some of the bandsmen were getting up and soon we heard the strains of 'Oh Come All Ye Faithful' and other carols, in the snow. This was done by the band as a surprise. So the next morning, Christmas Day 1918 we had only four miles to complete the march. On approaching the town quite a crowd had come out to see us march in, including a crowd of German girls. We looked at them, they looked at us and then one of our chaps took a rest. He bent down made up a snowball and threw it amongst the girls. They knew it was only done in fun and they quickly retaliated and soon we were in the midst of a snowball battle and that is how the Hampshire Regiment occupied the town of Merkermisk [Mechernich].[11] *(Pte George Watts, 2/4th Hampshires)*

The Hampshires were part of the 186th Brigade of the 62nd Division, the only Territorial Force formation to move into Germany on 15 December 1918, as part of the Rhine bridgehead force. Pte Watts, like many others, was billeted with a German family over the Christmas period:

> We went into a little back room and started our Christmas dinner (such as it was). The folk in the house were having their dinner of meat scraps and potatoes in the main room and the old lady kept coming and wanting us to come in with them but my mate was a bit awkward and said 'Why don't they leave us alone', but after a while, we went in with them. They had a Christmas tree and were trying to make merry. There was the old man of the house and his wife, four daughters and one son. I had a mouth organ and started playing 'The Merry Widow Waltz'. They knew that and were delighted. They got hold of us and danced round the Christmas tree and soon we were all friends (not enemies). This was to be our home until the first week of March. The weather kept frosty and bright. There was a large lake frozen over and we spent Sunday afternoons having fun on the lake sliding etc. Then there was tobogganing down a steep hill by moonlight.

Not everyone could boast of such an enjoyable time as some units were still on the move. In the Balkans the 26th Division moved into the Dobrudja region of Rumania. This area had been annexed by the Bulgarians in 1916 and British troops were now required to oversee the peaceful re-establishment of Rumanian rule over a population containing a sizeable minority of ethnic Bulgarians. The weather at this time was severe and many troops lacked adequate winter clothing, shortages being made up from local sources where possible. On the march with the Division was the 107th Field Company, working hard to maintain the poor roads and repair bridges destroyed over previous months by retreating German and Bulgarian troops:

> We did not know whether we would spend Xmas at Giurgiu or not. However, we determined to be as prepared as possible for it, and the surrounding villages were scoured for turkeys, geese etc. The turkeys cost about 40 lei, or about 22s, as compared with a peace time price of about 4s for a good large bird. Chickens, however, were a reasonable

price – about 1*s* 6*d* each. We got about seven turkeys, a duck, and eighteen chickens (the natives would not sell their geese) when, just a few days before Xmas, we received orders to embark on barges, to go down the Danube to Silistra. Our prospects for Xmas Day did not look very rosy, especially when we heard that we had to take three weeks' rations – iron rations of course – with us! However we brought our poultry with us – alive. Turkeys, 7; ducks, 1; chickens, 18; were taken on to the establishment of the Company and rationed accordingly.[12] (*Capt Melville Rattray*)

The sappers embarked on barges on 23 December and crossed the Danube to Rustchuk to draw rations. They spent Christmas Eve being towed along the river by a Bulgarian tugboat, arriving at Silistra at 1830 hrs:

Consequently . . . Xmas Day was to us an ordinary working day. Any attempt at properly celebrating the day would have to be carried out in adverse circumstances, for we were in the unsuitable condition of 'shifting', and making a new camp; everything was in an unsettled state, and there was plenty of work to do. Though we had the turkeys, we had nothing in which to roast them, and proper 'jollifications' could not be organized while we were busy unloading barges, making many journeys with equipment and three weeks' rations to our new camp, and settling down in it. Consequently it was decided to wait till we had got properly settled down, and to hold our 'Xmas' on New Year's Day. It was merely a postponement and not an abandonment of the event . . . Thus our first 'peace' Xmas – though we made up later – was as far as the actual date itself was concerned worse than our 'war' ones. It was just an ordinary working day, and bully beef was our Xmas fare – with no extras![13] (*Capt Melville Rattray*)

As the New Year approached, the Company, along with most of 79th Brigade, were well billeted in and around Silistra. More turkeys and even some geese had been purchased and a number of pianos, discovered in a former Bulgarian barracks, had been distributed among units, allowing evening sing-songs to take place. All now awaited their belated Christmas celebration when at 2300 hrs on New Year's Eve word came from 79th Brigade HQ to expect disturbances the following day:

Consequently, on New Year's morning all paraded with steel helmets, armed for all eventualities, and piled arms, ready to move at a moment's notice – an inauspicious start to the New Year of Peace! However, preparations for celebrating the day were not interrupted on that account, and all had a good 'Xmas' breakfast, remarking that it would be bad for any 'rioters' who disturbed them. As the day wore on and all was quiet, it became apparent that there was nothing doing in the 'disturbances' line, and the celebrations of the day were continued with. The annual Xmas football match between the Sappers and Drivers was played, and on this occasion the Sappers by no means had it all their own way, winning an even match by 1–0. Then all settled down to an excellent dinner of turkey, goose, plum pudding, beer, etc, and with a free issue of cigarettes and canteen goods, followed in the evening by a rum issue and a concert – accompanied on the piano – all spent an enjoyable day.[14] (*Capt Melville Rattray*)

Not all British troops in the territory of their former enemies were part of the occupation forces. In various locations men who had been prisoners of war were still awaiting repatriation. The poor transport network in places such as Anatolia in central Turkey and the vacuum left by the collapse of national and regional governments across the former Central Powers made the process of returning these men home a slow one. At Langensalza prisoner-of-war camp, between Mühlhausen and Erfurt in Germany, 2,000 British and a number of French prisoners had started on the journey of repatriation. Even so, this still left a large number of men facing Christmas in the camp:

As Christmas drew near an attempt was made to cheer us up somewhat and on the Sunday evening before Christmas there was a carol service in the church, the men joining heartily in the singing of carols. A Cpl of the Royal Artillery sang 'The Holy City' as a solo, the men joining in the chorus. Altogether it was a very helpful service and the hut was full. What the German sentry thought who stood outside I often wondered. The contrast on returning to the huts was great. There men were gambling, swearing and singing ribald songs. The service did not appeal to all the men and I overheard one NCO remark 'This after that!'

When Christmas day came it required a very big effort of will power to get the Christmas spirit and in spite of the Christmas morning service most felt terribly homesick, especially at the service, although two men in the choir very valiantly sang, 'Good King Wenceslaus', but somehow it all went flat. Nevertheless the group did its best afterwards to shake off the feeling, which like seasickness required an effort of will.

Just before the service a Russian came into our hut with a bottle in his arms that looked very much like a bottle of champagne and Paddy spotted it. The bottle was full and sealed and Paddy was determined to beat the Russian in a bargain over it and we all thought it would help in celebrating the Christmas dinner and so Paddy bargained. 'Hello Ruskie, what have you got there?' Ruskie, 'A bottle of champagne.' 'Don't believe you,' said Paddy, 'but anyhow what will you take for it?' 'A bar of soap,' said Ruskie. Soap was precious, 'Oh no,' said Paddy, 'I will give you a packet of tea.' The Russian refused but after a good deal of bargaining Paddy eventually got it for a ¼ lb tin of cocoa . . .

After the service on Christmas day we set to and prepared the Christmas dinner. There was plenty of food and the menu was:

> Stewed up pork and beans
> Maconochies Prepared Dinners
> Consisting of meat, potatoes, beans or peas and parsnips.
> Tinned ham or bully beef.
> Christmas Pudding.

The pudding was a great success the ingredients being boiled rice well mixed up with tinned rice and a spoonful or two of cocoa and sugar. It was not exactly Christmas pudding as generally understood but we succeeded in getting the colour right. Then came the champagne and the usual toasts, but when it was poured into our cups, although

Alten Grabow FC, a team comprising British prisoners of war from Alten Grabow Camp. This team played a match against an international prisoners' team on Monday 23 December 1918, as part of a four-day sports and general entertainments programme. *(8904-13)*

it fizzed all right we all felt suspicious and a tasting found it to be ordinary mineral water that could be obtained in the canteen. Poor Paddy. What he said about the Ruskie could not be written, but he swore by all saints that if he caught him he would boil him in mineral water. After dinner the afternoon was spent in walking it off round the camp and kicking a football about.

A concert in the evening and a quiet talk and read by a light, improvised out of dripping with a bit of rag soaked in the said dripping, and Christmas day was finished.

We were cheered up next morning with the news that another 2000 would leave camp on the Saturday. (*Rfm Harry Gore, 12th Rifle Brigade*)

The inmates of Langensalza camp were not alone in having dealings with Russians that winter. During 1918, the Allies had begun to commit troops to far-flung parts of the former Tsarist Empire in an attempt to curb German territorial ambitions and to secure large stockpiles of arms and munitions that had been sent to aid the Russian war effort. Once Germany

NCOs and men of a RAMC unit of the North Russia Expeditionary Force at Archangel in December 1918. They are wearing some of the warm clothing issued to troops in north Russia and Siberia to combat the harsh winter weather conditions. *(Q 17003)*

surrendered, the threat of their pre-eminence in the region was at an end. However, the Allied governments, rather than pull their forces out of Russia, became embroiled in a muddled and half-hearted attempt to support anti-Bolshevik 'White' forces. At the north Russian ports of Archangel and Murmansk could be found some 30,000 men, almost half of whom were British, under Gen Edmund Ironside. In south Russia former members of the British Salonika Force could be found at Sevastopol in the Crimea, Batoum in Georgia and even Baku on the Caspian Sea; the latter two locations being important for their oil. Troops from Mesopotamia were also involved in these operations, forming the largest contingent of the occupation force at Baku. Finally, there was a multinational Allied force, under Gen Alfred Knox, operating in Siberia along the Trans-Siberian Railway from the port of Vladivostok. For the troops in Siberia and northern Russia the harshness of the winter climate kept military operations to a minimum as the major battle was simply to keep warm:

20–28 November 1918: During this month the issue of warmer clothing was completed. Fur hats, leather jerkins, white canvas (Shackleton) boots, thick long stockings, index finger gloves, heavy mitts and heavy muffler were issued to all ranks. (*War Diary 2/7th Durham Light Infantry*)

At Omsk, in Siberia, temperatures by mid-December were down to 60°F of frost at midday (-28°C) and 79°F of frost at night (-47°C):

20 December 1918: Notwithstanding fullest preventative measures taken, several men suffering from frostbite. Anxiously awaiting further supplies of fur hats, mitts and boots, repeatedly asked for. (*War Diary 25th Middlesex*)

Under such conditions, preparations to celebrate Christmas became a key way to deflect the troops' minds from their current situation. In Siberia the war diary of the 25th Middlesex recalls difficulties in obtaining funds for regimental purposes and that the usual commodities associated with Christmas were not to be found, despite the best efforts of the British consul. But for the 2/7th DLI, with the North Russian Expeditionary Force, things were rather easier:

25 December 1918: At 12.45 a special dinner was provided for the Other Ranks by the Battalion. Five Roubles per man was allowed from the COs fund and five Roubles per man was also allowed by the War Office from NACB profits. In the evening at 19.00 a whist drive and sing song was arranged and later one parcel per other rank was provided from comforts sent by Queen Alexandra's Field Force Fund and other comforts held by the RASC . . .

The weather was not nearly so cold as had been anticipated. Some snow fell almost daily but on the level ground it was never over 2 ft deep. 26 pairs of skis were drawn by the Battalion. (*War Diary 2/7th DLI*)

At the same time as the DLI were engaged in their festivities a section of the 421st Battery, RFA, was on the move across the frozen landscape:

We were at Bakharitza opposite Archangel town when . . . two days before Christmas orders suddenly arrived for another section (2 gun) to proceed to the front. The centre section consisting of Maj Body, Lieut Hart and 58 other ranks entrained for Obozerskaya with guns, stores and ponies to form the 16th Brigade Canadian Field Artillery at Seletskoe 70 versts from Obozerskaya a three day march (march is just a term here). There was difficulty in loading beside the railway so a late start was for Volchenitya. There were difficulties and Volchenitya was reached late at night and was 11 o'clock before all were in. I wish I could show you the scene a forest clearing of about 2 acres, a great fire burning on the frozen riverbank and one or two of us dipping out water for the ponies. Volchenitya is described as three wooden huts. Maj Body says the men who took part in that march will not forget it when Christmas comes round they'll remember Christmas as spent in the snow-clad forest on the Seletskoe Obozerskaya trail. The forest dark and silent in the moonlight and all bustle and movement within, ponies and sledges constantly coming and going. There in one small clearing we were many nationalities Frenchmen (21st Colonial Infantry) who garrisoned the port, American hospital orderlies, British and Russian soldiers, men and women and children (drosky drivers) who all packed in together and thanking God for the roof overhead and fire, so Christmas 1918 was spent by Centre Section 421 Battery R.F.A. (*Gnr H.F. Goodright*)

In the Caucasus, weather conditions were more forgiving, although this had a drawback as local Bolsheviks could be more active, as occurred in Baku:

December 24 1918: Everyone confined to barracks as we are having a bit of trouble with the Bolsheviks, they have cut off our electric supply and threatened to attack our barracks, all guards are doubled and every patient in hospital fit to use a rifle served out with one. Things looking a bit ugly.

December 25 1918: Well Xmas Day, spending mine on guard, could be doing a lot worse I suppose.

December 26 1918: Sent some of our R.E.s to the power station under armoured car protection to see if they can put the electric plant in working order again.

December 27 1918: Electric on again, all troops standing by in case of trouble.

December 28 1918: Trouble with the people ended today so were allowed out again. (*Sgt William Dyer, 40th Field Ambulance, RAMC*)

At Batoum on the Black Sea, numbers of British troops were still arriving over the Christmas period. So, like the 107th Field Company in the Dobrudja, they could expect little but hard work until settled into billets:

We anchored 2 days before Christmas 1918. Everyone was anticipating to spend the Festival on board, but it was too good to be true . . . Sure enough we pulled alongside at Batoum on Xmas Eve and we knew what was going to happen. So we started unloading the horses first and the drivers took them away near an aerodrome. We gunners started unloading the guns, wagons, forage etc. We were handicapped as the weather was mucking. It was an all night job as we had brought over 90 days forage and iron rations and unfortunately rum. The unloading of both vessels took us up to Christmas Day at 6pm. Many gunners down the hole of the ship were drunk, having opened a case of rum. On being dismissed, at least before, the orderly bombardier warned me for night picquet with two others. So I thought just as well to finish off a Grand Christmas. (*Gnr Edmund Lenfestey, D Howitzer Battery, 27th Division, RFA*)

At Sevastopol, where men of the 3rd Royal Marine Light Infantry arrived on 9 December, all was quiet. The troops were quickly accommodated in the former Imperial Russian Naval Barracks and then had a chance to explore the city and sites relating to the Crimean War, although Christmas Day itself left much to be desired:

Dec 21st. Today I visited the Panorama of the Crimea War, it is one of the most wonderful pictures I ever saw everything is so real and life-like, in the grounds the Russians have some magnificent monuments erected in memory of those who fell.

Dec 25th. Another very happy Xmas day, we had a splendid spread of Bully and biscuits, my thoughts are very much at home.

Dec 27th. Station and magazine guards relieved by the French, they have now taken over command here and proclaimed Martial Law, anyone found loitering about after 9pm will be shot. This evening 2 of our Marines deserted taking with them their rifles and ammunition it is thought they have gone over to the Bolsheviks.

Dec 30th. Paraded 7.30am ready for marching off. Marched out of Naval Barracks Sebastopol 7.45 was detailed to proceed to Pier with my platoon to load lighters with provisions etc embarked on the ex-Bulgarian SS Dobruja 2pm. Left Sebastopol 2.30. (*Sgt Howard Couldrake, 3rd Royal Marine Light Infantry*)

Couldrake's unit returned to Mudros from where he embarked for England on 7 January 1919. Apart from troops slowly returning to Britain for demobilisation other soldiers could be found in the many military hospitals and army camps that had sprung up during the war through which thousands of men passed during their military service. In Burden Military Hospital, Weymouth, was found Pte Albert Bullock (8th Royal Warwicks) who had been wounded in the hip on 6 October 1918 during the battle to break the Hindenburg Line:

We were all told to put up a stocking on Christmas Eve but the Sister told me I should want a bedsock so Sweet put one up for me and it was full in the morning. I don't remember what I did have but I remember a box of 100 'Greys' as I thought it was Dr Bliss till Sweet told me they were from Nurse Beanell. We had a jolly good day I know and Jim came in at 2 p.m. and had dinner and tea with me and had supper with the staff and a bed. I couldn't thank Nurse Beanell as she sprained a ligament in her leg that night putting up some decorations and she was laid up for two months.

I was going well in the evening with a cigar when Devereaux came round. He was pleased to see me enjoying myself but said I wasn't to make myself sick with the cigar.

Christmas card produced by Reading War Hospital in 1918 to celebrate the festive season and the recently won peace. The card contains the following message from the officer in charge of the hospital, Col W.J. Maurice: *'At this, the fifth Christmas that we have spent in the midst of sorrow and suffering, let us be proud of our Country and our race: let us rejoice and be thankful that, through sacrifice, right has been victorious over wrong, and let us pray that, in due time, peace and good-will may reign amongst men.'* (2004-12-13)

At the Machine Gun Corps Training Camp at Grantham there was rather more 'festive spirit' flowing as the staff welcomed in 1919:

New Year's Eve found the Sergeants' Mess entertaining the officers; the officers providing the wine with which we toasted the New Year. The Sergeant Major went round filling as assortment of glasses and crockery, and failed to notice he missed the glass held by one Sergeant Nobby Clarke – a Scot. Somehow the officers heard of the omission next day and invited Nobby round to their mess. From his condition and amiability afterwards we gathered that our officers had done him proud. (*QMS Frederick Hunt, MGC*)

Postscript

When Christmas 1919 came around British and Dominion armed forces no longer constituted their 'nations in khaki' as they had been during the war. Churchill's revised demobilisation scheme had done its job, sending home long-serving volunteers. By November 1919, the British Army was reduced from 3.8 million men serving at the time of the armistice to 900,000. Although there were still occupation forces in Germany, the Tyrol and Turkey, as well as intervention forces in Russia, military forces of the British Empire were returning to something approaching their pre-1914 levels and roles. Those who had joined for 'the duration' were mostly to enjoy that family Christmas they had longed for during the years of conflict.

Christmas was then, and remains today, the most universal festival celebrated by the British. It is a time to be with one's family or, if this is not possible, a time when families and loved one are uppermost in one's thoughts. For soldiers, thrown into the largest and most destructive war fought up to that time, focus on the family through the sending and receipt of letters, cards and gifts, helped take their minds away from the reality of daily life in the front line, if only for a short time. Besides their immediate families, soldiers received evidence that they were not forgotten and that their service was valued by their local communities and individuals across the Empire, who sent Christmas gifts to serving soldiers through the many comfort committees or servicemen's support organisations that sprang up during the war.

For the Army too, the communal nature of Christmas celebrations lent themselves to unit-wide festivities. These were very important morale-boosting exercises with the men celebrating within their 'military family'.

Regimental and Territorial Force associations supported such activities and officers and NCOs went out of their way to provide the best food, drink and entertainment they could muster. The importance of such celebrations is indicated by the festivities being spread over the weeks surrounding 25 December. Whenever a unit was out of the front line it would find time to organise some sort of party. Indeed, wherever troops found themselves: in the muddy trenches of France and Flanders, in the deserts of the Middle East, among the ravines of Gallipoli or Macedonia, the mountains of Italy or the African bush, Christmas celebrations included traditional elements. A roast meal, including fowl if possible, presents, decorations, cards, concerts, general entertainments and sports were all on the checklist for a wartime Christmas. All were elements common to a peacetime celebration and as such brought some measure of familiarity and normality to men's lives as well as bringing members of a unit closer together.

Celebrations also crossed boundaries of nationality, in the European theatres of war at least, leading to British soldiers sharing festivities with Allied soldiers and civilians and on occasions even with the enemy. However, as this book has shown, instances of Christmas fraternisation with the enemy, from the large-scale truce of 1914 to the simple slackening of the intensity of warfare, did not undermine the British soldier's belief that the war had to be carried through to victory. This steadfastness remained although the troops were away from their homes and loved ones, often living in extremely adverse conditions, with the threat of death daily upon them. To sum up the attitude of the British Tommy one can do no better than to leave it to one of their own number:

I must write these special few lines to wish you all the Seasons Greetings, & every happiness & prosperity in the coming year. Am very sorry I cannot be with you all at this eventful season, such as never been the case before, for anyone of us to be away – but cheer-oh – drink & be merry, I shall be with you in spirit & thought.

Don't worry about me – I know where I should like to be, & *where I'm most comfortable*, but I also know where I'm most wanted, so out here with the lads I shall be enjoying myself likewise & thinking of the dear folk at home.[1] (*Pte Arthur Burke, 20th Manchesters*)

Notes

INTRODUCTION

1. Brown, M. and Seaton, S., *Christmas Truce – The Western Front 1914*.
2. For a detailed discussion of this see Ashworth, T., *Trench Warfare 1914– 1918 – the Live and Let Live System* (Pan Books, 2000).

THE FIRST CHRISTMAS: 1914

1. Letter to parents, dated 23 December 1914.
2. Letter to a Miss Francis, dated 13 December 1914.
3. Letter to his mother, dated 12 December 1914.
4. Figures from IWM website www. iwm.org.uk (page covering the whole story of Princess Mary's gift to the troops, Christmas 1914).
5. NA, WO 95/1441, War Diary, 4th Division Gen Staff, October– December 1914.
6. Letter to 'E G', dated 29 December 1914.
7. Letter to his parents, dated 27 December 1914.
8. Letter to his parents, dated 26 December 1914.
9. IWM Department of Documents, Ms letters of 2/Lt A.D. Chater, 2nd Gordon Highlanders.
10. NA, WO 95/154, War Diary, 1st Army Gen Staff, December 1914– March 1915 and WO 95/1627, War Diary, Gen Staff, 7th Division, October 1914–January 1915.
11. NA, WO 95/1441, War Diary, Gen Staff, 4th Division, October– December 1914.
12. *Ibid.*
13. Letter dated 31 December 1914.
14. Letter to his parents, dated 28 December 1914.
15. Letter to his parents and Len and Rene, dated 29 December 1914.
16. Letter to his parents and Len and Rene, dated 29 December 1914.
17. Letter to his mother and father, dated 29 December 1914.

18. NA, WO 95/5382, War Diary, Headquarters, West Africa – Cameroon, Report on Naval and Military Operations 1914–1916.

19. Unfortunately, the war diary of the 2nd Battalion, Nigeria Regiment (WO 95/5387) is incomplete and does not cover December 1914, so no other references to trucing were found.

20. NA, WO 95/5386, Lt Col Haywood's Papers – Reports and Correspondence, September 1914– April 1916.

21. NA, WO 95/5382, Report on the Operations of the Dschang Column, 21 December 1914–10 January 1915.

CHRISTMAS 1915

1. Entry for 6 December 1915 concerning the trenches around Festubert.

2. Letter to his mother, dated 16 December 1915.

3. Letter to mother, father and sisters, dated 13 December 1915.

4. Letter to his mother, dated 16 December 1915.

5. Letter to his mother, dated 9 January 1916.

6. Summary of Information No. 45: 6 a.m. 25th December – 6 a.m. 26th December 1915 in WO 95/2128: War Diary of 21st Division

General Staff, September–December 1915.

7. Letter to his mother and family, dated 26 December 1915.

8. NA, WO 95/2531: War Diary of the Headquarters, 111th Infantry Brigade, August 1915–April 1919.

9. Letter to his mother, dated 27 December 1915.

10. Letter to his father, dated 10 December 1915.

11. M.J. Rattray, *Three Years in the Balkans – Further Recollections of 107th Field Coy., R.E.*, p. 19.

12. Letter to his parents, dated 26 December 1915.

13. Letter to his mother, dated 26 December 1915.

14. Letter to his parents, dated 5 January 1916.

15. Letter to his parents, dated 25 December 1915.

16. Letter to Ellen, dated 22 December 1915.

CHRISTMAS 1916

1. Letter to his sister Bessie, dated 14 January 1917.

2. Letter to his brother Reg, dated 29 December 1916.

3. Letter to his wife, dated 25 December 1916.

4. Letter to his parents, dated 26 December 1916.

5. Letter to Lena and Gladys, dated 24 December 1916.

6. Letter to his mother and father, dated 21 December 1916.

7. Letter to his mother and father, dated 28 December 1916.

8. Letter to his family, dated 25 December 1916.

9. Letter to his family, dated 26 December 1916.

10. Letter to his sisters Enid and Mildred, dated 28 December 1916.

11. Letter to his wife, dated 7 January 1917, reproduced in J.M. Hammond, *A Living Witness*, p. 121.

12. Letter to his mother, dated 28 December 1916.

13. Barker, A., *Memories of Macedonia*, pp. 23–5.

14. Letter to Ellen, dated 3 January 1917.

CHRISTMAS 1917

1. Letter to his sister Bessie, dated 7 January 1918.

2. Letter to his brother Jack, dated 22 December 1917.

3. WO 95/1205: War Diary of the 76th Field Company, RE, 23 August 1915–March 1919.

4. Letter to his sister Maud, dated 30 December 1917.

5. Letter to his fiancée, dated 25 December 1917.

6. Letter to his parents, dated 25 December 1917.

7. From the diary of Pte A.V. Bullock.

8. From W. Mather, *'Muckydonia' 1917–1919 – Being the adventures of a one-time 'pioneer' in Macedonia and Bulgaria during the First World War*, p. 149

9. Letter to his mother dated 29 December 1917.

10. Letter to his parents, dated 1 January 1918.

11. Letter to his family, dated 16 December 1917.

12. Letter to his mother, dated 22–23 December 1917.

13. Letter to his mother, dated 30 December 1917.

14. Letter to his mother, dated 26 December 1917.

15. Letter to his father, dated 1 January 1918.

PEACE AT LAST! CHRISTMAS 1918

1. Letter to his mother, dated 29 December 1918.

2. Letter dated 28 December 1918.

3. Letter to his mother, dated 25 December 1918.

4. Letter to his mother, dated 25 December 1918.

5. Letter to his mother, dated 2 January 1919.

6. Letter to his mother, dated 24–25 December 1918.

7. Letter to his mother, dated 20 December 1918.

8. Letter to his fiancée Nell, dated 28 December 1918.

9. Letter to his wife, dated 12 January 1919.

10. Lt Col C. Wheeler (ed.), *Memorial Record of the Seventh (Service) Battalion The Oxfordshire and Buckinghamshire Light Infantry* (Blackwell, Oxford, 1921), pp. 165–6.

11. The battalion moved from Hellenthal to Kall on 24 December and marched to Mechernich on Christmas morning. Here they were to remain until 23 February when they moved to Wermelskirchen (reference from *2/4th Battalion Hampshire Regiment 1914–1918*, published by the battalion in late 1919).

12. M.J. Rattray, *Further Recollections of 107th Field Coy., R.E.*, p. 205.

13. *Ibid*, pp. 212–13.

14. *Ibid*, p. 216.

POSTSCRIPT

1. Letter to his mother and family, dated 25 December 1915.

Sources

UNPUBLISHED SOURCES

Brotherton Library, University of Leeds
Liddle Collection

GS 1700: Ms Letters, Pte Jack Webster, 10th Devons.

The National Archives

WO 95/4290: War Diary, Headquarters, The Royal Naval Division.

WO 95/154: War Diary, Gen Staff, 1st Army, December 1914–March 1915.

WO 95/1441: War Diary, Gen Staff, 4th Division, October 1914–December 1914.

WO 95/1627: War Diary, Gen Staff, 7th Division, October 1914–January 1915.

WO 95/2128: War Diary, Gen Staff, 21st Division, September 1915–December 1915.

WO 95/2427: War Diary, 21st Battalion, The Royal Fusiliers, November 1915–February 1916.

WO 95/2427: War Diary of the 1/4th Suffolks, November 1915–January 1916

WO 95/2731: War Diary of the 1/8th Londons, March 1915–January 1918.

WO 95/2531: War Diary, Headquarters, 111th Infantry Brigade, August 1915–April 1919.

WO 95/2611: War Diary, 14th Battalion, The Argyll & Sutherland Highlanders, June 1916–March 1919.

WO 95/5382: War Diary, Headquarters, West Africa – Cameroon: Report on Naval and Military Operations 1914–1916.

WO 95/5382: Report on the Operations of the Dschang Column, 21 December 1914–10 January 1915.

WO 95/5386: Lt-Col Haywood's Papers, Reports and Correspondence, September 1914–April 1916.

WO 95/5387: War Diary, 2nd Battalion, The Nigeria Regiment, August–September 1914 and July–September 1915.

National Army Museum
Department of Archives, Photographs, Film & Sound (APFS)

NAM 9802-214: Ts Diary, Capt Alfred E. Bundy, 2nd King's Own Royal Lancasters.

NAM 1986-11-43-7: Ts Account, Capt Keith F. Freeland, Indian Volunteer Artillery. This account is part of the Gallup Papers.

NAM 2003-10-28-2: Ms Account, Cpl Stanley Freeman, Royal Naval Division Signal Company.

NAM 1989-01-105-2: Ms Diary, Maj J.Q. Henriques, 1/16th Londons.

NAM 5603-11-3&4: Ms Journal of Lt Col Henry Jourdain, 5th Connaught Rangers.

NAM 1985-05-24-6: Ts Letter, Lt Col Rupert Shoolbred, 1/16th Londons. This letter is part of the Wilkin Papers.

NAM 1992-04-73-1: Ms Letters, Pte Richard Stratton, 15 Sanitation Section, RAMC.

NAM 2003-08-7: Ts Memoir, Pte George Veasey, 8th Ox & Bucks Light Infantry and 26th Middlesex.

Imperial War Museum
Department of Documents

92/36/1: Ms Letters, Pte Reg Bailey, 7th Royal Berkshires.

Con Shelf: Ms Letters, Capt Eric Barclay, 2nd and 4th Battalions The Nigeria Regiment.

73/140/1: Ms Diary, Lt Holroyd Birkett Barker, 134th Siege Battery, RGA.

Con Shelf: Ms Letters, Capt Charles Baxter, 6th South Lancashires.

94/5/1: Ms Diary, Pte Francis Victor Blunt, 2/15th Londons & 17 Training Depot Squadron, RAF.

82/21/1: Ts Memoir, Lt Frederick Arnold Brown, 7th Gloucesters (Sgt, 2nd Monmouthshires).

02/43/1: Ts Diary, Pte Albert Bullock, 8th Royal Warwicks.

Con Shelf: Ts Letters, Pte Arthur Burke, 20th Manchesters.

92/3/1: Ts Letters, Rfm Jack Chappell, 1/5th Londons.

87/56/1: Ms Letters, 2/Lt Dougan Chater, 2nd Gordon Highlanders.

88/11/1: Ts Letters, W.C. Christopher (letters of Gnrs Cecil and Ray Christopher, 47th Siege Battery, RGA).

88/52/1: Ts Memoir, Capt Sir George Clarke, 1/8th Londons.

87/62/1: Ms Letters, Lt Col Robert Clarke, 1/4th Royal Berkshires.

04/1/1: Ms Diary, Sgt Howard Couldrake, 3rd Royal Marine Light Infantry.

72/72/1: Ms & Ts Letters, Capt Eric de Normann, ASC.

P326: Ms Diaries, Pte David Doe, 51st Signal Company, RE.

87/56/1: Ts Memoir, 2/Lt Cyril Drummond, 32nd Brigade, RFA.

98/2/1: Ms Diary, Sgt William Gower Dyer, 40th Field Ambulance, RAMC.

98/28/1: Ms Diary & Memoir, Gnr Thomas G. Edgerton, D Battery, 301st Brigade, RFA.

67/256/1: Ts Letters, Lt J. Elliott, 3rd/6th King's African Rifles.

96/57/1: Ms Letters, Pte William Fall, 1st Entrenching Battalion, 2nd Canadian Division.

94/11/1: Ts Memoir, Cpl Bob Foulkes, 73rd Field Company, RE.

86/2/1: Ms Diaries, L/Cpl W.C. Gale, 2nd Norfolks.

87/45/1: Ts Letters, H.F. Goodright, 421st Battery, RFA.

01/36/1: Ts Memoir, Rfm Harry Gore, 12th Rifle Brigade.

84/9/1: Ts Letters, Rfm J. Selby Grigg, 1/5th Londons.

84/39/1: Ts Account (letter), Maj F.M. Hahn, 9th North Staffordshires.

02/35/1: Ms Letters, ACM Frank Haylett, Royal Flying Corps.

01/51/1: Ts Letters, Pte Harold Henfrey, 1/6th Lancashire Fusiliers.

03/31/1, Ts Memoir, Pte Christopher Hennessey, 2/15th Londons.

01/58/1: Ms Diaries, Gnr Ernest Hinchcliffe, RGA.

Con Shelf & 02/16/1: Ts Diary, Maj E.B. Hinde, 1/2nd East Anglian Field Ambulance, RAMC.

P253: Ms Diaries & Ts Transcription, Pte Walter Hoskyn, 5th King's Liverpools.

88/52/1: Ts Memoir, QMS Frederick Hunt, Machine Gun Corps.

02/29/1: Ts Memoir, Rfm J.A. Johnston, 13th Rifle Brigade.

97/5/1: Ms Letters, 2/Lt Winn William Johnstone-Wilson, 9th Royal Sussex.

04/20/1: Ms Letters, Capt Archibald Laporte-Payne, 175th Brigade, RFA.

99/13/1: Ms Letters, Pte Robert Lawson, 14th Argyll & Sutherland Highlanders.

91/22/1: Ms Diary, 2/Lt A.C.L.D. Lees, 2nd Battalion The Nigeria Regiment.

98/17/1: Ms Memoir, Gnr Edmund Lenfestey, D Howitzer Battery, 27th Division & 22nd Brigade, RFA..

98/2/1: Ts Memoir, Pte Alfred W. Lewis, 6th Northamptons

86/66/1: Ts Letters, Rfm Richard Lintott, 1/5th Londons.

87/26/1: Ms Diary, David Lloyd-Burch, 10th Field Ambulance, RAMC.

80/25/1: Ts Letters, Lt Joseph McPherson, Camel Transport Corps.

02/16/1: Ts Letters, Capt James Mackie, 2/4th Somerset Light Infantry.

01/53/1 & 1A: Ts Letters, Pte Mowbray Meades, 2nd Middlesex.

93/25/1: Ms Letters, Rfm Ernest Morley, 1/16th Londons.

Con Shelf: Ms Letters, Roland Mountfort, 25th Royal Fusiliers.

02/4/1: Ms Letters & Memoir, Pte Fred Philipson, 1st Grenadier Guards.

79/9/1: Ms Transcriptions of Letters, Capt Conrad Price, 2nd Norfolks.

92/19/1, Ms Letters, 2/Lt Charles Philip Quayle, 1/16th Londons.

79/35/1: Ms & Ts Memoir, Pte W.A. Quinton, 2nd Bedfords.

02/39/1: Ms Diary, Pte Thomas Rainbird, 1st West Yorkshires.

96/23/1: Ms Letters, Lt Emrys Richards, 63rd Battalion, MGC.

96/23/1: Ts Diary, 2/Lt Harold Hyde Ridsdale, 76th Field Company, RE.

74/98/1: Ts Memoir: Spr Frank Rowland, Royal Engineers (Signals).

02/55/1: Ms Letters, Spr Jim Sams, Royal Engineers.

DS/MISC/44: Microfilm Ts Letters, Capt Mervyn Sibly, 9th Gloucesters.

87/56/1: Ms Letters, 2/Lt Wilbert Spencer, 2nd Wiltshires.

81/1/1: Ms Account, Pte William Tate, 2nd Coldstream Guards.

87/17/1: Ms Diary, Capt Eustace Vachell, 6th Field Company, RE.

88/61/1: Ms Diary, Brig Gen Sir Richard Wapshare.

89/7/1: Ts Memoir, Gnr Fred Warburton, RFA.

01/38/1: Ts Memoir, Pte George Watts, 2/4th Hampshires.

97/17/1: Ms Diary & Ts Transcription, Pte Henry White, 1/5th The Queens (Royal West Surrey Regiment).

Con Shelf: Ms Letters, Pte George Wilkinson, 10th Royal Fusiliers.

97/18/1: Ms Letters, Capt Herbert Ewart Winn, 2/5th Gurkhas.

83/12/1: Ms Diaries & Ts Transcript, Capt James Digby Wyatt, 2/4th Gloucesters.

01/47/1: Ms Letters, Gnr William Young, 175 Siege Battery, RGA.

Royal Air Force Museum
Department of Research & Information Services (DoRIS)

X003-0380/002, Ms Letters, Air Mechanic 3 John Roscoe, 20 Training Depot
Squadron, RAF.

PUBLISHED SOURCES

Barker, A., *Memories of Macedonia*, Arthur H. Stockwell, London, *c.* 1918.

Brown, M. and Seaton, S., *Christmas Truce – The Western Front, December 1914*, Pan
Books, London, 1999.

Hammond, J.M., *A Living Witness – Letters of John Maximilian Hammond MB, BS, DSO,
1914–1918*, Morgan & Scott, London, 1925.

Mather, W., *'Muckydonia' 1917–1919 – Being the adventures of a one-time 'pioneer' in
Macedonia and Bulgaria during the First World War*, Ilfracombe, 1979.

Rattray, M.J., *Three Years in the Balkans – Further Recollections of the 107th Field Coy,
R.E.*, William Dresser, Darlington, 1920.

Wheeler, Lt-Col C. (ed.), *A Memorial Record of the Seventh (Service) Battalion The
Oxfordshire & Buckinghamshire Light Infantry*, Blackwell, Oxford, 1921.

Articles from the *Inglewood Advertiser*

Letter home dated 25 December 1916 from Dvr Alan Gillespie, 2nd Ammunition
Sub-Park Transport, AIF, reproduced in the column 'Tidings of Soldiers', 20 March
1917.

Letter to his mother dated 27 December 1915, Pte Frank Scholes, 14th Battalion, AIF,
reproduced in the column 'Tidings of Soldiers', 11 February 1916.

Index

Note: **Bold** page numbers indicate photographs, and captions to photographs.